CW00547450

letters
of
mahatma
gandhi

letters
of
mahatma
gandhi

RUPA

Published by
Rupa Publications India Pvt. Ltd 2019
7/16, Ansari Road, Daryaganj
New Delhi 110002

Sales centres:
Allahabad Bengaluru Chennai
Hyderabad Jaipur Kathmandu
Kolkata Mumbai

Copyright © Rupa Publications India Pvt. Ltd 2019

All rights reserved.
No part of this publication may be reproduced, transmitted,
or stored in a retrieval system, in any form or by any means,
electronic, mechanical, photocopying, recording or otherwise,
without the prior permission of the publisher.

ISBN: 978-93-5333-676-9

First impression 2019

10 9 8 7 6 5 4 3 2 1

Printed at HT Media Ltd., Gr. Noida

This book is sold subject to the condition that it shall not,
by way of trade or otherwise, be lent, resold, hired out, or otherwise
circulated, without the publisher's prior consent, in any form
of binding or cover other than that in which it is published.

Contents

Leo Tolstoy

The legendary Russian author Leo Tolstoy (1828–1910), who wrote such masterpieces as *War and Peace* and *Anna Karenina*, profoundly influenced generations of thinkers after him, including Mahatma Gandhi. Their long correspondence, which began after Gandhi read a copy of Tolstoy's *Letter to a Hindu* while in South Africa, is invaluable in studying the history and genealogy of such influence.

1

To Leo Tolstoy
Westminster Palace Hotel,
4, Victoria Street,
London, S.W.,
1 October, 1909

Sir,

I take the liberty of inviting your attention to what has been going on in the Transvaal (South Africa) for nearly three years.

There is in that colony a British Indian population of nearly 13,000. These Indians have for several years laboured under the various legal disabilities. The prejudice against colour and in some respect against Asiatics is intense in that colony. It is largely due, so far as Asiatics are concerned, to trade jealousy. The climax was reached three years ago, with a law which I and many others considered to be degrading and calculated to unman those to whom it was applicable. I felt that submission to law of this nature was inconsistent with the spirit of true religion. I and some of my friends were and still are firm believers in the doctrine of non-resistance to evil. I had the privilege of studying your writings also, which left a deep impression on my mind. British Indians, before whom the position was fully explained, accepted the advice that we should not submit to the legislation, but that we should suffer imprisonment, or whatever other penalties the law may impose for its breach. The result has been that nearly one-half of the Indian population that was unable to stand the heat of the struggle, to suffer the hardships of imprisonment, have withdrawn from the Transvaal rather than submit to law which they have considered degrading. Of the other half, nearly 2,500 have for conscience's sake allowed themselves to be imprisoned, some as many as five times. The imprisonments have varied from four days to six months; in the majority of cases with hard labour. Many have been financially ruined. At present there are over hundred passive resisters in the Transvaal goals. Some of these have been very poor men, earning their livelihood from day to day. The result has been that their wives and children have had to be supported out of public contributions, also largely raised from passive resisters. This has put a severe strain upon British Indians, but in my opinion they have risen to the occasion. The struggle still continues and one does not know when the end will come. This, however, some of us at least have seen most clearly, that passive resistance will and can succeed where brute force must fail. We also notice that in so far as the struggle has been prolonged, it has been due largely to our weakness, and hence to a belief having been engendered in the mind of the Government that we would not be able to stand continued suffering.

Together with a friend, I have come here to see the imperial authorities and to place before them the position, with a view to seeking redress. Passive resisters have recognized that they should have nothing to do with pleading with the Government, but the deputation has come at the instance of the weaker members of the community, and it therefore represents their weakness rather than their strength. But in the course of my observation here, I have felt that if a general competition for an essay on the Ethics and Efficacy of Passive Resistance were invited, it would popularize the movement and make people think. A friend has raised the question of morality in connection with the proposed competition. He thinks that such an invitation would be inconsistent with the true spirit of passive resistance, and that it would amount to buying opinion. May I ask you to favour me with your opinion on the subject of morality? And if you consider that there is nothing wrong in inviting contributions, I would ask you also to give me the names of those whom I should specially approach to write upon the subject.

There is one thing more, with reference to which I would trespass upon your time. A copy of your letter addressed to a Hindu on the present unrest in India has been placed in my hands by a friend. On the face of it, it appears to represent your views. It is the intention of my friend, at his own expense, to have 20,000 copies printed and distributed and to have it translated also. We have, however, not been able to secure the original, and we do not feel justified in printing it, unless we are sure of the accuracy of the copy and of the fact that it is your letter. I venture to enclose herewith a copy of the copy, and should esteem it a favour if you kindly let me know whether it is your letter, whether it is an accurate copy and whether you approve of its publication in the above manner. If you will add anything further to the letter please do so. I would also venture to make a suggestion. In the concluding paragraph you seem to dissuade the reader from the belief in reincarnation. I do not know whether (if it is not impertinent on my part to mention this) you have specially studied the question. Reincarnation or transmigration is a cherished belief with millions in India, indeed in China also. With many one might almost say it is a matter of experience, no longer a matter of academic acceptance. It explains reasonably the many mysteries of life. With some of the passive resisters who have gone through the gaols of the Transvaal, it has been their solace.

My object in writing this is not to convince you of the truth of the doctrine, but to ask you if you will please remove the word 'reincarnation' from the other things you have dissuaded your reader from. In the letter in question you have quoted largely from Krishna and given reference to passages. I should thank you to give me the title of the book from which the quotations have been made.

I have wearied you with this letter. I am aware that those who honour you and endeavour to follow you have no right to trespass upon your time, but it is rather their duty to refrain from giving you trouble, so far as possible. I have, however, who am an utter stranger to you, taken the liberty of addressing this communication in the interests of truth, and in order to have your advice on problems, the solution of which you have made your life work.

With respects, I remain,

Your obedient servant,
M.K. Gandhi

2

Yasnaya Polyana,
7 October, 1909

M.K. Gandhi
Transvaal

Just now I have received your very interesting letter, which gives me great pleasure. May God help all your dear brothers and co-workers in the Transvaal. This fight between gentleness and brutality, between humility and love on one side, and conceit and violence on the other, makes itself ever more strongly felt here to us also—especially in the sharp conflicts between religious obligations and the laws of the State expressed by the conscientious objection to render military service. Such objections are taking place very frequently.

I have written *A Letter to a Hindu* and am very pleased to have it translated (into English). The title of the book on Krishna will be communicated to you from Moscow. As regards rebirth I, for my part, shall leave out nothing; for, as it appears to me, the belief in a rebirth will never be able to strike such deep roots in and restrain mankind as the belief in the immortality of the soul and the faith in divine truth and love; of course I would accommodate you, if you so desire, to delete those passages in question. It will give me great pleasure to help your edition. Publication and circulation of my writings, translated into Indian dialects, can only be a matter of pleasure to me.

The question regarding monetary payment of Royalty should not at all be allowed to appear in religious undertakings.

I give my fraternal greetings and am glad to have come
into personal contact with you.

Leo Tolstoy

3

Dear Sir,

I beg to tender my thanks for your registered letter in connection with the letter addressed to a Hindu, and with the matters that I dealt with in my letter to you.

Having heard about your failing health I refrained, in order to save you the trouble from sending an acknowledgement, knowing that a written expression of my thanks was a superfluous formality; but Mr Aylmer Maude whom I have now been able to meet reassured me that you are keeping good health indeed and that unfailingly and regularly you attend to your correspondence every morning. It was very gladsome news to me and it encourages me to write to you further about matters which are, I know, of the greatest importance according to your teaching.

I beg to send you herewith a copy of a book written by a friend—an Englishman—who is at present in South Africa, in connection with my life, in so far it has a bearing on the struggle with which I am so connected and to which my life is dedicated. As I am very anxious to engage your active interest and sympathy I thought that it would not be considered by you as out of the way for me to send you the book.

In my opinion, this struggle of the Indians in the Transvaal is the greatest of modern times, inasmuch as it has been idealized both as to the goal as also to the methods adopted to reach the goal. I am not aware of a struggle in which the participators are not to derive any personal advantage at the end of it and in which 50 per cent of the persons affected have undergone great suffering and trial for the sake of a principle. It has not been possible for me to advertise the struggle as much as I should like. You command, possibly, the widest public today. If you are satisfied as to the facts you will find set forth in Mr Doke's book, and if you consider that the conclusions I have arrived at are justified by the facts, may I ask you to use your influence in any manner you think fit to popularize the movement? If it succeeds, it will be not only as a triumph of religion, love and truth over irreligion, hatred, and falsehood but it is highly likely to serve as an example to the millions in India and to people in other parts of the world, who may be down-trodden and will certainly go a great way towards breaking up the party of violence, at least in India. If we hold out to the end, as I think we would, I entertain not the slightest doubt as to its ultimate success and your encouragement in the way suggested by you can only strengthen us in our resolve.

The negotiations that are going on for a settlement of the question have practically fallen through, and together with my colleagues I return to South Africa this week and invite imprisonment. I may add that my son has happily joined me in the struggle and is now undergoing imprisonment with hard labour for six months. This is his fourth imprisonment in the course of the struggle.

If you would be so good as to reply to this letter, may I ask you to address your reply to me at Johannesburg, S.A., Box 6522.

Hoping that this will find you in good health,
I remain,

Your obedient servant,
M.K. Gandhi

4

Dear Sir,

You may remember that I have written to you from London where I stopped temporarily. As your devoted follower I send you herewith a brief booklet which I have written. I have translated my own writings from Gujarati (my own language). What is remarkable is that my original book was confiscated by the Government of India. Therefore I was in a hurry to publish this translation. I am afraid I am burdening you; but if your health permits and you have time to go through my booklet, then I need not express how greatly I shall value your criticism of it. I am sending also a few copies of your *A Letter to a Hindu* which you allowed me to publish. This letter will also be translated into an Indian dialect.

Yours respectfully,
M.K. Gandhi

5

Dear Friend,

Just now I have received your letter and your book, *Indian Home Rule*.

I have read your book with great interest, because I think the question you have therein dealt with is important not only for Indians, but for the whole of Mankind.

I cannot find your first letter, but by discovering your biography by Doke, I happen to know you through that biography which gripped me and it gave a chance to know and understand you better.

I am not very well at present. So I am unable to write to you on all the questions which are interconnected with your book and also with your activities in general, which I value much. But I shall write to you as soon as I recover.

Your friend and brother,
Leo Tolstoy

6

21–24, Court Chambers,
Johannesburg,
15 August, 1910

To
Count Leo Tolstoy

Dear Sir,

I am much obliged to you for your encouraging and cordial letter of the 8th May last. I very much value your general approval of my booklet, *Indian Home Rule*. And if you have the time, I shall look forward to your detailed criticism of the work which you have been so good as to promise in your letter.

Mr Kallenbach has written to you about Tolstoy Farm. Mr Kallenbach and I have been friends for many years. I may state that he has gone through most of the experiences that you have so graphically described in your work *My Confession*. No writing has so deeply touched Mr Kallenbach as yours; and, as a spur to further effort in living up to the ideals held before the world by you, he has taken the liberty, after consultation with me, of naming his farm after you.

Of his generous action in giving the use of the farm for passive resisters, the numbers of *Indian Opinion* I am sending herewith will give you full information.

I should not have burdened you with these details but for the fact of your taking a personal interest in the passive resistance struggle that is going on in Transvaal.

I remain,

Your faithful servant,
M.K. Gandhi

7

To
M.K. Gandhi,
Johannesburg,
Transvaal, South Africa

'Kotechety.'[1]
7 September, 1910

I have received your Journal *Indian Opinion* and I am happy to know all that is written on non-resistance. I wish to communicate to you the thoughts which are aroused in me by the reading of those articles.

The more I live—and specially now that I am approaching death, the more I feel inclined to express to others the feelings which so strongly move my being, and which, according to my opinion, are of great importance. That is, what one calls non-resistance, is in reality nothing else but the discipline of love undeformed by false interpretation. Love is the aspiration for communion and solidarity with other souls, and that aspiration always liberates the source of noble activities. That love is the supreme and unique law of human life, which everyone feels in the depth of one's soul. We find it manifested most clearly in the soul of the infants. Man feels it so long as he is not blinded by the false doctrines of the world.

That law of love has been promulgated by all the philosophies—Indian, Chinese, Hebrew, Greek and Roman. I think that it had been most clearly expressed by Christ, who said that in that law is contained both the law and the

---

[1]Castle of Tolstoy's eldest daughter.

Prophets. But he has done more; anticipating the deformation to which that law is exposed, he indicated directly the danger of such deformation which is natural to people who live only for worldly interests. The danger consists precisely in permitting one's self to defend those interests by violence; that is to say, as he has expressed, returning blow by blows, and taking back by force things that have been taken from us, and so forth. Christ knew also, just as all reasonable human beings must know, that the employment of violence is incompatible with love, which is the fundamental law of life. He knew that, once violence is admitted, doesn't matter in even a single case, the law of love is thereby rendered futile. That is to say that the law of love ceases to exist. The whole Christian civilisation, so brilliant in the exterior, has grown up on this misunderstanding and this flagrant and strange contradiction, sometimes conscious but mostly unconscious.

In reality as soon as resistance is admitted by the side of love, love no longer exists and cannot exist as the law of existence; and if the law of love cannot exist, there remains no other law except that of violence, that is the right of the mighty. It was thus that the Christian Society has lived during these nineteen centuries. It is a fact that all the time people were following only violence in the organization of Society. But the difference between the ideals of Christian peoples and that of other nations lies only in this: that, in Christianity the law of love had been expressed so clearly and definitely as has never been expressed in any other religious doctrine; that the Christian world had solemnly accepted that law, although at the same time it had permitted the employment of violence and on that violence it had constructed their whole life. Consequently, the life of the Christian peoples is an absolute contradiction between their profession and the basis of their life, contradiction between love recognized as the law of life, and violence recognized as inevitable in different departments of life: like Governments, Tribunals, Army, etc. which are recognized and praised. That contradiction developed with the inner development of the Christian world and has attained its paroxysm in recent days.

At present the question poses itself evidently in the following manner: either it must be admitted that we do not recognize any discipline, religious or moral, and that we are guided in the organization of life only by the law of force, or that all the taxes that we exact by force, the judicial and police organizations and above all the army must be abolished.

This spring in the religious examination of a secondary school of girls in Moscow, the Professor of Catechism as well as the Bishop had questioned the young girls on the Ten Commandments and above all on the sixth 'Thou shalt not kill'. When the examiner received good reply, the Bishop generally paused for another question: Is killing proscribed by the sacred Law always and in all cases? And the poor young girls perverted by their teachers must reply: No, not always; killing is permitted during war, and for the execution of criminals. However one of those unfortunate girls (what I relate is not a fiction but a fact that has been transmitted to me by an eye-witness), having been asked the same question, 'Is killing always a crime?' was moved deeply, blushed and replied with decision, 'Yes, always.' To all the sophisticated questions habitual to the Bishop she replied with firm conviction: killing is always forbidden in the Old Testament as well as by Christ who not only forbids killing but all wickedness against our neighbours. In spite of all his oratorical talent and all his imposing grandeur, the Bishop was obliged to beat a retreat and the young girl came out victorious.

Yes, we can discuss in our journals the progress in aviation and such other discoveries, the complicated diplomatic relations, the different clubs and alliances, the so-called artistic creations, etc. and pass in silence what was affirmed by the young girl. But silence is futile in such cases, because every one of this Christian world is feeling the same, more or less vaguely, like that girl. Socialism, Communism, Anarchism, Salvation army, the growing criminalities, unemployment and absurd luxuries of the rich, augmented without limit, and the awful misery of the poor, the terrible increasing number of suicides— all these are the signs of that inner contradiction which must be there and which cannot be resolved; and without doubt, can only be resolved by acceptation of the law of Love and by the rejection of all sorts of violence. Consequently your work in Transvaal, which seems to be far away from the centre of our world, is yet the most fundamental and the most important to us supplying the most weighty practical proof in which the world can now share and with which must participate not only the Christians but all the peoples of the world.

I think that it would give you pleasure to know that with us in Russia, a similar movement is also developing rapidly under the form of the refusal of military services augmenting year after year. However small may be the number of your participators in non-resistance and the number of those in Russia who refuse military service, both the one and the other may assert with audacity that 'God is with us' and that 'God is more powerful than men'.

Between the confession of Christianity, even under the perverted form in which it appears amongst us Christian peoples, and the simultaneous recognition of the necessity of armies and of the preparation for killing on an ever-increasing scale, there exists a contradiction so flagrant and crying that sooner or later, probably very soon, it must invariably manifest itself in utter nakedness; and it will lead us either to renounce the Christian religion, and to maintain the governmental power or to renounce the existence of the army and all the forms of violence which the state supports and which are more or less necessary to sustain its power. That contradiction is felt by all the governments, by your British Government as well as by our Russian Government; and therefore, by the spirit of conservatism natural to these governments, the opposition is persecuted, as we find in Russia as well as in the articles of your journal, more than any other anti-governmental activity. The governments know from which direction comes the principal danger and try to defend themselves with a great zeal in that trial not merely to preserve their interests but actually to fight for their very existence.

With my perfect esteem,
Leo Tolstoy

G.K. Gokhale

Gopal Krishna Gokhale (1866–1915) was a senior leader of the Indian National Congress in its early days. He was an educationist and a social reformer, who founded the Servants of India Society at Poona in 1905, and visited South Africa in 1912 on Gandhiji's invitation.

1

21–24, Court Chambers,
Corner, Rissik & Anderson Street,
P. O. Box 6522,
Johannesburg,
13 January, 1905

To
The Honourable Professor Gokhale,
Poona
Dear Professor Gokhale,

The existence of *Indian Opinion* you know. It has now embarked on a career when I think I may fairly appeal to you for active sympathy. I propose to write perfectly frankly, as you know me too well to misunderstand me. When I saw that Mr Madanjit could not carry on the paper without pecuniary assistance and as I knew that he was guided by thoroughly patriotic motives, I placed at his service the bulk of my savings. That, however, was not enough. Three months ago I took over the whole responsibility and management. Mr Madanjit still remains nominally the proprietor and publisher, because I believe that he has done much for the community. My own office is at present being worked in the interest of *Indian Opinion* and I have already become responsible to the extent of nearly £3,500. Some English friends, who knew me intimately and before whom I placed the scheme as described in the enclosed, took up the idea and now it is in full working order and, although it does not show the same measure of self-sacrifice as shown by the founders of the Fergusson College in Poona, I venture to think that it is not a bad copy. It has been a most delightful thing to me to see the English friends coming forward so boldly. They are not literary men but they are sterling, honest, independent men. Each of them had his own business or employment where he was doing well, and yet none of them had the slightest hesitation in coming forward as a worker for a bare living which means £3 per month, with a distant prospect of getting profits.

It is also my intention, if my earnings continue, to open a school on the grounds, which would be second to none in South Africa for the education primarily of Indian children who would be resident boarders, and secondarily, of all who want to join the school but would also reside on the premises. For this, too, volunteer workers are required. It would be possible to induce one or two Englishmen and English ladies here to give their lifetime to this work, but Indian teachers are absolutely necessary. Could you induce any graduates who have an aptitude for teaching, who bear a blameless character and who would be prepared to work for a mere living? Those who would come must be well-tried, first-class men. I would want two or three at least but more could certainly be accommodated, and after the school is in working order, it is intended to add a sanatorium with open-air treatment on hygienic lines. My immediate purpose, however, is in connection with *Indian Opinion*. If you approve of all I have said regarding it, will you kindly send a letter of encouragement to be sent to the editor for publication; also if you could spare a few moments, occasionally write an article ever so small for it? I am also anxious to secure either honorary or paid correspondents who would contribute weekly notes in English, Gujarati, Hindi and Tamil. If it becomes expensive, I might have to be satisfied with only English correspondence which would lend itself to being translated in the three Indian languages. Could you recommend any such correspondent or correspondents? The weekly notes should give an idea of what is being done on your side with reference to the Indian question, giving extracts from notices of the question in the newspapers, and should contain matters that are likely to be interesting to the Indians in South Africa. You may at your discretion disclose partly or wholly the contents of this letter in so far as such a course may be necessary in the interests of the subject-matter hereof. I hope you are keeping good health.

I remain,

Yours faithfully,
M.K. Gandhi

2

Dear Mr Gokhale,

For the time being I am at Cape Town watching the course of events. I do not want to inflict on you any news as about the struggle. I shall be as brief as I possibly can.

Mr Andrews and Mr Pearson are truly good men, we all like them very much. Sir Benjamin has disappointed us. He has hardly done any good and he may do a great deal of harm. He is weak and by no means sincere. Even now he has hardly grasped the details.

And he undoubtedly, consciously or unconsciously, fosters divisions among us. Mr Andrews will tell you all about him. But I thought that I should give you my impressions of Sir Benjamin.

If there is a settlement in March, I propose to leave for India in April. I shall have with me probably about twenty men, women and children who will live with me. These will include the school children who are likely to come. I do not know whether you still want me to live at the Servants of India quarters in Poona or how. I shall be prepared to do so immediately after I have paid a visit to the members of my family. It is likely that the number living with me may be augmented by some members of my family who may wish to share my life and work. Please do not consider yourself bound to keep me at the Society's quarters. I am entirely in your hands. I want to learn at your feet and gain the necessary experience. No matter whether I am staying somewhere under your guidance or not, I shall scrupulously observe the compact of silence for one year after my arrival in India. The vow of silence as I have understood it does not include the South African question and may be broken at your wish for furthering any project about which both of us hold the same view.

My present ambition you know. It is to be by your side as your nurse and attendant. I want to have the real discipline of obeying someone whom I love and look up to. I know I made a bad secretary in South Africa. I hope to do better in the Motherland if I am accepted.

May you benefit in health by the change and the calmer atmosphere on the continent.

This letter will be in your hands about the middle of March. If you deem it necessary to say anything to me about my movements, you will of course cable. I assume too that you will not want me to go to Poona before you return. If you did, I should of course go.

If I am enabled to leave for India in April, I propose to use the funds you have sent for our passages which shall be all deck. I have no means of my own and Phoenix can hardly supply funds now. It is drained totally dry.

I remain,

Yours faithfully,
M.K. Gandhi

C.F. Andrews

C.F. Andrews (1871–1940) was a Christian missionary and social reformer who met Gandhiji in South Africa, after being sent there by G.K. Gokhale to act as a mediator between the government and the local Indian community. He subsequently became one of Gandhiji's closest friends, championing his cause. Dubbed 'Christ's Faithful Apostle' by Gandhiji, he wrote three books on the Mahatma.

1

My Dear Charlie,

I have your letters. I prize them. They give me only partial consolation. My difficulties are deeper than you have put them. All you raise I can answer. I must attempt in this letter to reduce my own to writing. They just now possess me to the exclusion of everything else. All the other things I seem to be doing purely mechanically. This hard thinking has told upon my physical system. I hardly want to talk to anybody. I do not want even to write anything, not even these thoughts of mine. I am therefore falling back upon dictation to see whether I can clearly express them. I have not yet reached the bottom of my difficulties, much less have I solved them. The solution is not likely to affect my immediate work. But of the failure I can now say nothing. If my life is spared I must reach the secret somehow.

You say: 'Indians as a race did repudiate it, bloodlust, with full consciousness in days gone by and deliberately took their choice to stand on the side of humanity.' Is this historically true? I see no sign of it either in the Mahabharata or the Ramayana, not even in my favourite Tulsidas which is much superior in spirituality to Valmiki. I am not now thinking of these works in their spiritual meanings. The incarnations are described as certainly bloodthirsty, revengeful and merciless to the enemy. They have been credited with having resorted to tricks also for the sake of overcoming the enemy. The battles are described with no less zest than now, and the warriors are equipped with weapons of destruction such as could be possibly conceived by the human imagination. The finest hymn composed by Tulsidas in praise of Rama gives the first place to his ability to strike down the enemy... Then take the Mahomedan period. The Hindus were not less eager than the Mahomedans to fight. They were simply disorganized, physically weakened and torn by internal dissensions. The code of Manu prescribes no such renunciation that you impute to the race. Buddhism, conceived as a doctrine of universal forbearance, signally failed, and, if the legends are true, the great Shankaracharya did not hesitate to use unspeakable cruelty in banishing Buddhism out of India. And he succeeded! Then the English period. There has been compulsory renunciation of arms but not the desire to kill. Even among the Jains the doctrine has signally failed. They have a superstitious horror of blood (shed), but they have as little regard for the life of the enemy as a European. What I mean to say is that they would rejoice equally with anybody on earth over the destruction of the enemy. All then that can be said of India is that individuals have made serious attempts, with greater success than elsewhere, to popularize the doctrine. But there is no warrant for the belief that it has taken deep root among the people.

You say further: 'My point is that it has become an unconscious instinct, which can be awakened any time as you yourself have shown.' I wish it was true. But I see that I have shown nothing of the kind. When friends told me here that passive resistance was taken up by the people as a weapon of the weak, I laughed at the libel, as I called it then. But they were right and I was wrong. With me alone and a few other co-workers it came out of our strength and was described as Satyagraha, but with the majority it was purely and simply passive resistance what they resorted to, because they were too weak to undertake methods of violence. This discovery was forced on me repeatedly in Kaira. The people here being comparatively freer, talked to me without reserve, and told me plainly that they took up my remedy because they were not strong enough to take up the other, which they undoubtedly held to be far more manly than mine. I fear that the people whether in Champaran or in Kaira would not fearlessly walk to the gallows or stand a shower of bullets and yet say, in one case, 'we will not pay the revenue', and in the other, 'we will not work for you'. They have it not in them. And I contend that they will not regain the fearless spirit until they have received the training to defend themselves. Ahimsa was preached to man when he was in full vigour of life and able to look his adversaries straight in the face. It seems to me that full development of body-force is a sine qua non of full appreciation and assimilation of Ahimsa.

I do agree with you that India with her moral force could hold back from her shores any combination of armies from the West or the East or the North or the South. The question is, how can she cultivate this moral force? Will she have to be strong in body before she can understand even the first principles of this moral force? This is how millions blaspheme the Lord of the Universe every morning before sunrise.

'I am changeless Brahma, not a collection of the five elements—earth, etc.—I am that Brahma whom I recall every morning as the Spirit residing in the innermost sanctuary of my heart, by whose grace the whole speech is adorned, and whom the Vedas have described as—"Neti, neti".'

I say we blaspheme the Lord of the Universe in reciting the above verse because it is a parrot recitation without any consideration of its grand significance. One Indian realizing in himself all that the verse means is enough to repel the mightiest army that can approach the shores of India. But it is not in us today and it will not come until there is an atmosphere of freedom and fearlessness on the soil. How to produce that atmosphere? Not without the majority of the inhabitants feeling that they are well able to protect themselves from the violence of man or beast. Now I think I can state my difficulty. It is clear that before I can give a child an idea of moksha, I must let it grow into full manhood. I must allow it to a certain extent to be even attached to the body, and then when it has understood the body and so the world around it, may I easily demonstrate the transitory nature of the body and the world, and make it feel that the body is given not for the indulgence of self but for its liberation. Even so must I wait for instilling into any mind the doctrine of Ahimsa, i.e., perfect love, when it has grown to maturity by having its full play through a vigorous body. My difficulty now arises in the practical application of the idea. What is the meaning of having a vigorous body? How far should India have to go in for a training in arms-bearing? Must every individual go through the practice or is it enough that a free atmosphere is created and the people will, without having to bear arms, etc., imbibe the necessary personal courage from their surroundings? I believe that the last is the correct view, and, therefore, I am absolutely right as things are in calling upon every Indian to join the army, always telling him at the same time that he is doing so not for the lust of blood, but for the sake of learning not to fear death. Look at this from Sir Henry Vane. I copy it from Morley's *Recollections* (Vol. II):

Death holds a high place in the policy of great communities of the world... It is the part of a valiant and generous mind to prefer some things before life, as things for which a man should not doubt, nor fear to die.... True natural wisdom pursueth the learning and practice of dying well, as the very end of life, and indeed he hath not spent his life ill that hath learnt to die well. It is the chiefest thing and duty of life. The knowledge of dying is the knowledge of liberty, the state of true freedom, the way to fear nothing, to live well, contentedly, and peaceable... It is a good time to die when to live is rather a burden than a blessing, and there is more ill in life than good.

'When his hour came, Vane's actual carriage on Tower Hill was as noble and resolute as his words' is Morley's commentary. There is not a single recruiting speech in which I have not laid the greatest stress upon this part of a warrior's duty. There is no speech in which I have yet said, 'Let us go to kill the Germans.' My refrain is, 'Let us go and die for the sake of India and the Empire', and I feel that, supposing that the response to my call is overwhelming and we all go to France and turn the scales against the Germans, India will then have a claim to be heard and she may then dictate a peace that will last. Suppose further that I have succeeded in raising an army of fearless men, they fill the trenches and with hearts of love lay down their guns and challenge the Germans to shoot them—their fellow men—I say that even the German heart will melt. I refuse to credit it with exclusive fiendishness. So it comes to this, that under exceptional circumstances, war may have to be resorted to as a necessary evil, even as the body is. If the motive is right, it may be turned to the profit of mankind and that an ahimsaist may not stand aside and look on with indifference but must make his choice and actively co-operate or actively resist.

Your fear about my being engrossed in the political strife and intrigues may be entirely set aside. I have no stomach for them, least at the present moment, had none even in South Africa. I was in the political life because there through lay my own liberation. Montagu said, 'I am surprised to find you taking part in the Political life of the country!' Without a moment's thought I replied, 'I am in it because without it I cannot do my religious and social work,' and I think the reply will stand good to the end of my life.

You can't complain of my having given you only a scrap of a letter. Instead of a letter, I have inflicted upon you what may almost read like an essay. But it was necessary that you should know what is passing in my mind at the present moment. You may now pronounce your judgement and mercilessly tear my ideas to pieces where you find them to be wrong.

I hope you are getting better and stronger. I need hardly say that we shall all welcome you when you are quite able to undertake a journey.

With love,
Mohan

2

This letter was prompted by the contemporary reception of Rabindranath Tagore's speech in Tokyo, where he warned Japan against imitating the West. The speech was met with derision, and this was Gandhiji's response.

[Nadiad],
29 July, 1918

My Dear Charlie,

I must indulge myself again. I begin to perceive a deep meaning behind the Japanese reluctance to listen to the message of a Prophet from a defeated nation. War will be always with us. There seems to be no possibility of the whole human nature becoming transformed. Moksha and Ahimsa [are] for individuals to attain. Full practice of Ahimsa is inconsistent with possession of wealth, land or rearing of children. There is a real Ahimsa in defending my wife and children even at the risk of striking down the wrongdoer. It is perfect Ahimsa not to strike him but intervene to receive his blows. India did neither on the field on Plassey. We were a cowardly mob warring against one another, hungering for the Company's silver and selling our souls for a mess of pottage. And so have we remained more or less—more rather than less—up to today. There was no Ahimsa in their miserable performance, notwithstanding examples of personal bravery and later corrections of the exaggerated accounts of those days. Yes, the Japanese reluctance was right. I do not know sufficiently what the fathers of old did. They suffered, I expect, not out of their weakness, but out of their strength. The rishis of old stipulated that their religious practices were to be protected by the

Kshatriyas. Rama protected Vishwa-mitra from the rakshasas disturbing his meditations. He could later on dispense with this protection. I find great difficulties in recruiting but do you know that not one man has yet objected because he would not kill. They object because they fear to die. This unnatural fear of death is mining the nation. For the moment, I am simply thinking of the Hindus. Total disregard of death in a Mahomedan lad is a wonderful possession.

I have not written a coherent letter today but I have given you indications of my mental struggle.

Do you know that Sorabji is dead. He died in Johannesburg. A life full of promise has come to an abrupt end. The ways of God are inscrutable.

With deep love,

Yours,
Mohan

3

My Dear Charlie,

You have written to me more or less regularly but owing to your wanderings, I have not known where to write. Your latest has given me a deliberate address. I hope therefore this will reach you safely wherever you may be.

I have read your article in the *New Republic*. I am not taking it in *Y.I.* [*Young India*] It is therefore being sent to Brelvi as you have desired.

The events have moved fairly fast. I see as clearly as never before that the spirit of violence must be dealt with by non-violent action if the situation is to be at all saved. There is the growing violence of the Government expressing itself in a variety of ways—the subtle exploitation and the necessary prosecutions as a consequence of that exploitation for instance. You will note the extended meaning I have given to violence. Greed, pilfering, untruth, crooked diplomacy—all these are phases or signs or results of violent thought and action. The reaction of this violence upon the thinking educated people is remarkable and daily growing. I have therefore to deal with this double violence. To sit still at this juncture is stupid if not cowardly. I have made up my mind to run the boldest risks. I have arrived at this definite conclusion as a result of deep and prayerful thinking. Lahore revealed it all to me. The nature of the action is not yet clear to me. It has to be civil disobedience. How it is to be undertaken and by whom besides me I have not yet seen quite clearly. But the shiny cover that over-lays the truth is thinning day by day and will presently break.

I hardly wanted to write this when I begin this letter. But there you are.

Gurudev passed delightful two hours with me. He has aged considerably. We came nearer each other this time and I was so thankful. We had fully intended to meet again but Bomanji suddenly took him away to Baroda.

Manilal and his wife and baby are here. Ramdas has already. He is in Bardoli assisting Vallabhbhai's work. Mahadev is just now here.

We did not get your first volume from the publishers. I asked the *Young India* people to purchase a copy. It is on my desk at present. I have read the first chapter. It is a fair representation of my religious attitude.

Love,
Mohan

Rabindranath Tagore

Gurudev Rabindranath Tagore (1861–1941), arguably India's most renowned littérateur and definitely one of its greatest, maintained a long and famous association with Gandhiji, through periods of great political and cultural upheaval, even though they were not always in agreement politically. The correspondence that follows amply demonstrates why these two great minds were—inevitably—drawn to collaborate with each other.

1

[Bombay]
5 April, 1919

Dear Gurudev,

This is an appeal to you against our mutual friend, Charlie Andrews. I have been pleading with him for a message from you for publication in the national struggle which, though in form it is only directed against a single piece of legislation, is in reality a struggle for liberty worthy of a self-respecting nation. I have waited long and patiently. Charlie's description of your illness made me hesitate to write to you personally. Your health is a national treasure and Charlie's devotion to you is superhuman. It is divine and I know that if he could help it he would not allow a single person, whether by writing or his presence, to disturb your quiet and rest. I have respected this lofty desire of his to protect you from all harm. But I find that you are lecturing in Benaras. I have, therefore, in the light of this fact corrected Charlie's description of your health which somewhat alarmed me and I venture to ask you for a message from you—a message of hope and inspiration for those who have to go through the fire. I do it because you were good enough to send me your blessings when I embarked upon the struggle. The forces arrayed against me are, as you know, enormous. I do not dread them, for I have an unquenchable belief that they are supporting untruth and that if we have sufficient faith in truth, it will enable us to overpower the former. But all forces work through human agency.

I am therefore anxious to gather round this mighty struggle the ennobling assistance of those who approve it. I will not be happy until I have received your considered opinion on this endeavour to purify the political life of the country. If you have seen anything to alter your first opinion of it, I hope you will not hesitate to make it known. I value even adverse opinions from friends, for though they may not make me change my course, they serve the purpose of so many lighthouses to give out warnings of dangers lying in the stormy paths of life. Charlie's friendship has been to me on this account an invaluable treasure, because he does not hesitate to share with me even his unconsidered notes of dissent. This I count a great privilege. May I ask you to extend at this critical moment the same privilege that Charlie has?

I hope that you are keeping well and that you have thoroughly recuperated after your fatiguing journey through the Madras Presidency.

Yours sincerely,
M.K.G.

2

Dear Mahatmaji,

Power in all its forms is irrational—it is like the horse that drags the carriage blindfolded. The moral element in it is only represented in the man who drives the horse. Passive resistance a force which is not necessarily moral in itself, it can be used against truth as well as for it. The danger inherent in all force grows stronger when it is likely to gain success, for then it becomes temptation.

I know your teaching is to fight against evil by the help of the good. But such a fight is for heroes and not for men led by impulses of the moment. Evil on one side naturally begets evil on the other, injustice leading to violence and insult to vengefulness. Unfortunately such a force has already been started, and either through panic or through wrath our authorities have shown us the claws whose sure effect is to drive some of us into the secret path of resentment and others into utter demoralization. In this crisis you, as a great leader of men, have stood among us to proclaim your faith in the ideal which you know to be that of India, the ideal which is both against the cowardliness of hidden revenge and the cowed submissiveness of the terror-stricken. You have said, as Lord Buddha has done in his time and for all time to come—*Akkodhena jine kodham, asadhum sadhuna jine*—'Conquer anger by the power of non-anger and evil by the power of good.'

This power of good must prove its truth and strength by its fearlessness, by its refusal to accept any imposition which depends for its success upon its power to produce frightfulness and is not ashamed to use its machines of destruction to terrorize a population completely disarmed. We must know that moral conquest does not consist in success, that failure does not deprive it of its dignity and worth. Those who believe in spiritual life know that to stand against wrong which has overwhelming material power behind it is victory itself—it is the victory of the active faith in the ideal in the teeth of evident defeat.

I have always felt, and said accordingly, that the great gift of freedom can never come to a people through charity. We must win it before we can own it. And India's opportunity for winning it will come to her when she can prove that she is morally superior to the people who rule her by their right of conquest. She must willingly accept her penance of suffering— the suffering which is the crown of the great. Armed with her utter faith in goodness she must stand unabashed before the arrogance that scoffs at the power of spirit.

And you have come to your motherland in the time of her need to remind her of her mission, to lead her in the true path of conquest, to purge her present day politics of its feebleness which imagines that it has gained its purpose when it struts in the borrowed feathers of diplomatic dishonesty.

This is why I pray most fervently that nothing that tends to weaken our spiritual freedom may intrude into your marching line, that martyrdom for the cause of truth may never degenerate into fanaticism for mere verbal forms, descending into the self-deception that hides itself behind sacred names.

With these few words for an introduction allow me to offer the following as a poet's contribution to your noble work:

I

Let me hold my head high in this faith that thou art our shelter, that all fear is mean distrust of these. Fear of man? But what man is there in this world, what king, King of kings, who is thy rival, who has hold of me for all time and in all time and in all truth? What power is there in this world to rob me of my freedom? For do not thy arms reach the captive through the dungeon-walls, bringing unfettered release to the soul? And must I cling to this body in fear of death, as a miser to his barren treasure? Has not this spirit of mine the eternal call to thy feast of everlasting life? Let me know that all pain and death are shadows of the moment; that the dark force which sweeps between me and thy truth is but the mist before the sunrise; that thou alone art mine forever and greater than all pride of strength that dares to mock my manhood with its menace.

II

Give me the supreme courage of love, this is my prayer—the courage to speak, to do, to suffer at thy will, to leave all things or be left alone. Give me the supreme faith of love, this is my prayer—the faith of the life in death, of the victory in defeat, of the power hidden in the frailness of beauty, of the dignity of pain that accepts hurt, but disdains to return it.

Very sincerely yours,
Rabindranath Tagore

3

Dear Gurudev,

This is early morning 3 o'clock of Tuesday. I enter the fiery gate at noon. If you can bless the effort, I want it. You have been to me a true friend because you have been a candid friend often speaking your thoughts aloud. I had looked forward to a firm opinion from you one way or the other. But you have refused to criticize. Though it can now only be during my fast, I will yet prize your criticism, if your heart condemns my action. I am not too proud to make an open confession to my blunder, whatever the cost of the confession, if I find myself in error. If your heart approves of the action I want your blessing. It will sustain me. I hope I have made myself clear.

My love

M.K. Gandhi

Y.C.P.

20–9–'32

10.30 a.m.

Just as I was handing this to the Superintendent, I got your loving and magnificent wire. It will sustain me in the midst of the storm I am about to enter. I am sending you a wire.

Thank you.

M.K.G.

4

Mahatmaji,

Our people are wonderstruck at the impossible being made possible in these few days and there is a universal feeling of immense relief at your being saved for us. Now is the opportune moment when a definite command from you will rouse the Hindu community to make a desperate effort to win over Mohamedans to our common cause. It is even more difficult of success than your fight against untouchability, for there is a deep rooted antipathy against the Muslims in most of our people and they also have not much love for ourselves. But you know how to move the hearts of those that are obdurate, and only you, I am sure, have the patient love that can conquer the hatred that has accumulated for ages. I do not know how to calculate political consequences but I believe that nothing can be too costly which would enable us to win their confidence and convince them that we understand their difficulties and their own point of view. However, it is not for me to advise you and I shall fully rely upon your own judgement as to the course that should be taken. Only one suggestion I must venture to make to you that you might ask the Hindu Maha Sabha to make a conciliatory gesture towards the other party.

I have no doubt that you are gaining strength and inspiring every moment strength and hope around you.

With reverent love,
I am,
Ever yours,
Rabindranath Tagore

5

Yeravada Central Prison (Poona),
[9 October, 1932]

Dear Gurudev,

I have your beautiful letter. I am daily seeking light. This unity between Hindus and Muslims is also life's mission. The restrictions too hamper me. But I know that when I have the light, it will pierce through the restrictions. Meanwhile I pray though I do not yet fast.

I hope you were none the worse for the strenuous work in Poona and equally fatiguing long journey.

Mahadev translated for us your beautiful sermon to the villagers on the 20th ultimo. With love

Yours,
M.K. Gandhi
9–10–'32
Y.C.P.

6

Visva-Bharati,
Santiniketan, Bengal,
15 November, 1932

Dear Mahatmaji,

I can realize the sanctity of the promise given by you to Kelappan, and certainly nobody from outside can presume to criticize any actions that you may decide upon guided by your own direct revelation of truth. What I fear is that following so close upon the tremendous impact made on our consciousness by the recent fast a repetition of it may psychologically be too much for us properly to evaluate and effectively to utilize for the uplift of humanity. The mighty liberating forces set in motion by your fast still continue to operate and spread from village to village, removing age-long iniquities, transforming the harshness of the callously superstitious to a new feeling of sympathy for the distressed. Were I convinced that the movement has suffered any abatement or in any way shows signs of lacunae, I would welcome even the highest sacrifice which humanity today is capable of making, the sacrifice of your life in penance for our sins. But all my experiences, of the activities of the villages around us here, as well as of other localities, convince me that the movement generated by your fast continue to gain in strength and conquer formidable obstacles. The testimony of my friends from all parts of India confirm this truth. It may be that there are reactionary elements but it seems to me that we should allow them time—the pressure of a growing public opinion is sure to win them over. Even as to the Guruvayyur temple if my information is correct, excepting a few misguided individuals, the majority of men is overwhelmingly on the side of reform. I pray and hope that the former will yet yield to sanity and constitutionally remove the legal barriers which seem to stand in the way of reform. Should we take too seriously the activities of some isolated groups of individuals and subject millions of our countrymen to the extremest form of suffering while they themselves are unquestionably on the side of truth? The influence which is at work may have a check if anything happens to you. Should we risk that possibility now that we have won? These are the thoughts which naturally rise in my mind and I was thinking of putting them before Mahadev when your letter arrived. I shall continue to follow events with my thoughts and prayers and fervently hope that those who now stand in the way of truth will be converted to it.

With reverent love,
Yours,
Rabindranath Tagore

7

Dear Gurudev,

Your previous letter comforts me. It is enough for me that you are watching and praying.

    With deep love,

Yours,
M.K.G.
24–11-'32

8

Dear Gurudev,

I have read your press message regarding the Yeravda Pact, in so far as it applied to Bengal. It caused me deep grief to find that you were misled by very deep affection for me and by your confidence in my judgement into approving of a Pact which was discovered to have done a grave injustice to Bengal. It is now no use my saying that affection for me should not have affected your judgement out or that, confidence in my judgement ought not to have made you accept a Pact about which you had ample means for coming to an independent judgement. Knowing as I do your very generous nature, you could not have acted otherwise than you did and in spite of the discovery made by you that you have committed a grave error you would continue to repeat such errors if the occasions too were repeated.

But I am not at all convinced that there was any error made. As soon as the agitation for an amendment of the Pact arose I applied my mind to it, discussed, it with friends who ought to know and I was satisfied that there was no injustice done to Bengal. I corresponded with those who complained of injustice. But they too, including Ramanand Babu, could not convince me of any injustice. Of course our points of view were different. In my opinion, the approach to the question was also wrong.

A Pact arrived at by mutual arrangement cannot possibly be altered by the British Government except through the consent of the parties to the Pact. But no serious attempt seems to have been made to secure any such agreement. Your appearance, therefore, on the same platform as the complainants, I, for one, welcome, in the hope that it could lead to a mutual discussion, instead of a futile appeal to the British Government. If, therefore, you have, for your own part, studied the subject and have arrived at the opinion that you have now pronounced, I would like you to convene a meeting of the principal parties and convince them that a grave injustice has been done to Bengal. If it can be proved, I have no doubt that the Pact will be reconsidered and amended so as to undo the wrong, said to have been done to Bengal. If I felt convinced that there was an error of judgement, so far as Bengal was concerned, I would strain every nerve to see that the error was rectified. You may know that up to now I have studiously refrained from saying anything in public, in defence of the Pact save by way of reiterating my opinion, accompanied by the statement that if injustice could be proved, redress would be given. I am, therefore, entirely at your service.

Just now, I am absorbed in disbanding the Ashram and devising means of saving as much as can be for public use. My service will, therefore, be available after I am imprisoned which event may take place any day after the end of this month. I hope you are keeping good health.

Yours sincerely,
M.K. Gandhi

9

Dear Gurudev,

The All-India Village Industries Association which is being formed under the auspices of the Indian National Congress will need the assistance of expert advisers in the various matters that will engage its attention. It is not intended to trouble them to meet together or even the members of the Association but merely to advise the Association whenever reference is made to them in matters in which they possess special knowledge, e.g., in chemical analysis, food values, sanitation, distribution of village manufactures, improved methods of developing village industries, co-operation, disposal of village waste as manure, methods of village transport, education (adult and other), care of infants, and many other things too numerous to mention here.

Will you please allow your name to appear among such advisers of the All-India Village Industries Association? Naturally I approach you in the belief that the object of the Association and the method of approach to its task have your approval.

Yours sincerely,
M.K. Gandhi

10

Dear Gurudev,

I have just received your letter of 5th inst. Had I not to go to Belgaum on the very date you will have the opening ceremony, I would most certainly have come not only for the ceremony but also to see you and Santiniketan which I have not seen now for years. As it is I shall be with you in spirit when Jawaharlal will be performing the ceremony. May the Chinese Hall be a symbol of living contact between China and India.

The letter you wrote to me over that momentary misunderstanding lies in my jacket as a treasure. It brought tears of joy to my eyes. It was so worthy of you. With love and respects,

Yours,
M.K. Gandhi
Segaon,
Wardha,
9–4-'37

11

Dear Gurudev,

Your precious letter is before me. You have anticipated me.
I wanted to write as soon as Sir Nilratan sent me his last
reassuring wire. But my right hand needs rest. I did not want
to dictate. The left hand works slow. This is merely to show
you what love some of us bear towards you. I verily believe
that the silent prayers from the hearts of your admirers have
been heard and you are still with us. You are not a mere singer
of the world. Your living word is a guide and an inspiration
to thousands. May you be spared for many a long years yet
to come.

 With deep love,

Yours sincerely,
M.K. Gandhi
Segaon, Wardha,
23–9-'37

12

'Uttrayan'
Santiniketan, Bengal
19 February, 1940

Dear Mahatmaji,

You have just had a bird's-eye view this morning of our Visva-Bharati centre of activities. I do not know what estimate you have formed of its merit. You know that though this institution is national in its immediate aspect it is international in its spirit, offering according to the best of its means India's hospitality of culture to the rest of the world.

At one of its critical moments you have saved it from an utter breakdown and helped it to its legs. We are ever thankful to you for this act of friendliness.

And, now before you take your leave of Santiniketan I make my fervent appeal to you. Accept this institution under your protection, giving it an assurance of permanence if you consider it to be a national asset. Visva-Bharati is like a vessel which is carrying the cargo of my life's best treasure, and I hope it may claim special care from my countrymen for its preservation.

I hope we shall be able to keep close to a reticent expression of love and reverence in welcoming you into our Ashram and never allow it to overflow into any extravagant display of phrases. Homage to the great naturally seeks its manifestation in the language of simplicity, and we offer you these few words to let you know that we accept you as our own and as one who belongs to all humanity.

Just at this moment there are problems that darken our

destiny. These, we know are crowding your path and none of us is free from their attack. Let us for a while pass beyond the bounds of this turmoil and make our meeting today a simple meeting of hearts whose memory will remain when all the moral confusions of our distracted politics will be allayed and the eternal value of all our true endeavours will be revealed.

With love,
Rabindranath Tagore

13

On the way to Calcutta,
19 February, 1940

Dear Gurudev,

The touching note that you put into my hands as we parted has gone straight into my heart. Of course Visva-Bharati is a national institution. It is undoubtedly also international. You may depend upon my doing all I can in the common endeavour to assure its permanence. I look to you to keep your promise to sleep religiously for about an hour during the day.

Though I have always regarded Santiniketan as my second home, this visit has brought me nearer to it than ever before.

With reverence and love,

Yours,
M.K. Gandhi

Jawaharlal Nehru

Not only is Jawaharlal Nehru (1889–1964) Gandhiji's most famous apprentice (even though, over time, he diverted significantly from Gandhiji in his political views), it would not be hyperbolic to say that Bapu and Pandit Nehru were two of the primary architects of Independent India. Their long collaboration, both during the freedom struggle and in developing the very structure of the Indian subcontinent as we know it today, is the stuff of history. The following letters offer significant insight into their friendship.

1

The first phase of mass jailing in response to the Non-Co-operation Movement began in December 1921. Tens of thousands were prosecuted and imprisoned on technicalities. At the time of the infamous Chauri Chaura incident, both Jawaharlal Nehru and his father Motilal Nehru were in jail, prompting Gandhiji to call off the Movement. This letter from Gandhiji was read aloud to the imprisoned Nehru by Vijaylakshmi Pandit.

Bardoli,
19 February, 1922

My Dear Jawaharlal,

I see that all of you are terribly cut up over the resolutions of the Working Committee. I sympathize with you, and my heart goes out to Father. I can picture to myself the agony through which he must have passed, but I also feel that this letter is unnecessary because I know that the first shock must have been followed by a true understanding of the situation. Let us not be obsessed by Devidas's youthful indiscretions. It is quite possible that the poor boy has been swept off his feet and that he has lost his balance, but the brutal murder of the constables by an infuriated crowd which was in sympathy with Non-co-operation cannot be denied. Nor can it be denied that it was politically minded crowd. It would have been criminal not to have heeded such a clear warning.

I must tell you that this was the last straw. My letter to the Viceroy was not sent without misgivings as its language must make it clear to anyone. I was much disturbed by the Madras doings, but I drowned the warning voice. I received letters both from Hindus and Mohammedans from Calcutta, Allahabad and the Punjab, all these before the Gorakhpur incident, telling me that the wrong was not all on the Government side, that our people were becoming aggressive, defiant and threatening, that they were getting out of hand and were not non-violent in demeanour. Whilst the Ferozepur Jirka incident is discreditable to the Government, we are not altogether without blame. Hakimji complained about Bareilly. I have bitter complaints about Jajjar. In Shahajanpur too there has been a forcible attempt to take possession of the Town Hall. From Kanouj to the Congress Secretary himself telegraphed saying that the volunteer boys had become unruly and were picketing a High School and preventing youngsters under sixteen from going to the school. 36,000 volunteers were enlisted in Gorakhpur, not one hundred of whom conformed to the Congress pledge. In Calcutta Jamnalalji tells me there is utter disorganization, the volunteers wearing foreign cloth and certainly not pledged to non-violence. With all this news in my possession and much more from the South, the Chauri Chaura news came like a powerful match to ignite the gunpowder, and there was a blaze. I assure you that if the thing had not been suspended we would have been leading not a non-violent struggle but essentially a violent struggle. It is undoubtedly true that non-violence is spreading like the scent of the otto of roses throughout the length and breadth of the land, but the foetid smell of violence is still powerful, and it would be unwise to ignore or underrate it. The cause will prosper by this retreat. The movement had unconsciously drifted from the right path. We have come back to our moorings, and we can again go straight ahead. You are in as disadvantageous a position as I am advantageously placed for judging events in this due proportion.

May I give you my own experience of South Africa? We had all kinds of news brought to us in South Africa in our jails. For two or three days during my first experience I was glad enough to receive tit-bits, but I immediately realized the utter futility of interesting myself in this illegal gratification. I could do nothing, I could send no message profitably, and I simply vexed my soul uselessly. I felt that it was impossible for me to guide the movement from the Jail. I therefore simply waited till I could meet those who were outside and talk to them freely, and then too I want you to believe me when I tell you that I took only an academic interest because I felt it was not my province to judge anything, and I saw how unerringly right I was. I well remember how the thoughts I had up to the time of my discharge from the jail on every occasion were modified immediately after discharge and after getting first-hand information myself. Somehow or other the jail atmosphere does not allow you to have all the bearings in your mind. I would therefore like you to dismiss the outer world from your view altogether and ignore its existence. I know this is a most difficult task, but if you take up some serious study and some serious manual work you can do it. Above all, whatever you do, don't you be disgusted with the spinning wheel. You and I might have reason to get disgusted with ourselves for having done many things and having believed many things, but we shall never have the slightest cause for regret that we have pinned our faith to the spinning wheel or that we have spun so much good yarn per day in the name of the motherland. You have the Song Celestial with you. I cannot give you the inimitable translation of Edwin Arnold, but this is the rendering of the Sanskrit text. 'There is no waste of energy; there is no destruction in this. Even a little of this Dharma saves one from many a pitfall.' 'This Dharma' in the original refers to Karma Yoga, and the Karma Yoga of our age is the spinning wheel. I want a cheering letter from you after the freezing dose you have sent me through Pyarelal.

Yours sincerely,
M.K. Gandhi

2

My Dear Jawaharlal,

I must dictate and save time and give rest to my aching shoulder.
I wrote to you on Sunday about Fenner Brockway. I hope you
got that letter in due time.

Do you know that it was because you were the chief partner
in the transactions referred to that I wrote the articles you
have criticized, except of course about the so-called 'All India
Exhibition'? I felt a kind of safety that in view of the relations
between you and me my writings would be taken in the spirit in
which they were written. However I see that they were a misfire
all round. I do not mind it. For, it is evident that the articles
alone could deliver you from the self-suppression under which
you have been labouring apparently for so many years. Though I
was beginning to detect some differences in viewpoint between
you and me, I had no notion whatsoever of the terrible extent
of these differences. Whilst you were heroically suppressing
yourself for the sake of the nation and in the belief that by
working with and under me in spite of yourself, you would
serve the nation and come out scatheless, you were chafing
under the burden of this unnatural self-suppression. And, while
you were in that state, you overlooked the very things which
appear to you now as my serious blemishes. I could show you
from the pages of *Young India* equally strong articles written
by me, when I was actively guiding the C., with reference
to the doings of the All India Congress Committee. I have
spoken similarly at the All India Congress Committee meetings

whenever there has been irresponsible and hasty talk or action. But whilst you were under stupefaction these things did not jar on you as they do now. And it seems to me therefore useless to show you the discrepancies in your letter. What I am now concerned with is future action.

If any freedom is required from me I give you all the freedom you may need from the humble, unquestioning allegiance that you have given to me for all these years and which I value all the more for the knowledge I have now gained of your state. I see quite clearly that you must carry on open warfare against me and my views. For, if I am wrong I am evidently doing irreparable harm to the country and it is your duty after having known it to rise in revolt against me. Or, if you have any doubt as to the correctness of your conclusions, I shall gladly discuss them with you personally. The differences between you and me appear to me to be so vast and radical that there seems to be no meeting ground between us. I can't conceal from you my grief that I should lose a comrade so valiant, so faithful, so able and so honest as you have always been; but in serving a cause, comradeships have got to be sacrificed. The cause must be held superior to all such considerations. But this dissolution of comradeship—if dissolution must come in no way affects our personal intimacy. We have long become members of the same family, and we remain such in spite of grave political differences. I have the good fortune to enjoy such relations with several people. To take Sastri for instance, he and I differ in the political outlook as poles asunder, but the bond between him and me that sprung up before we knew the political differences has persisted and survived the fiery ordeals it had to go through.

I suggest a dignified way of unfurling your banner. Write

to me a letter for publication showing your differences. I will print it in *Young India* and write a brief reply. Your first letter I destroyed after reading and replying to it, the second I am keeping, and if you do not want to take the trouble of writing another letter, I am prepared to publish the letter that is before me. I am not aware of any offensive passage in it. But if I find any, you may depend upon my removing every such passage. I consider that letter to be a frank and honest document.

With love,
Bapu

3

My Dear Jawaharlal,

Instead of guiding the Dhami people I have passed them on to you. I feel that you should discharge this burden without any interference from me. The idea in the States seems to be to isolate and ignore the Congress and hence the States' Conference. I have already suggested in *Harijan* that no State association or mandal should act on its own without reference to your committee. I should act, if at all, through you, i.e. when you refer to me, I should give my opinion as I do in respect of the W.C. I told the Gwalior people also likewise yesterday. You will have to reorganize your committee a bit, if it is to function properly.

After all I could not go to Kashmir. Sheikh Abdulla and his friends won't tolerate the idea of my being State guest. Banking on my past experience, I had accepted State offer in anticipation of Sheikh Abdulla's approval. But I saw that I was mistaken. I therefore cancelled the acceptance of the State hospitality and accepted the Sheikh's. This embarrassed the State. So I cancelled the visit altogether. I was guilty of double stupidity in daring to think of going there without you and in not getting Sheikh's permission before accepting the State offer. I had thought that I would serve the people by accepting the State offer. I must confess that I was not pleased with my contact [with] the Sheikh and his friends. They seemed to all of us to be most unreasonable. Khan Saheb reasoned with them. But it was to no purpose.

Your visit to Ceylon was glorious. I don't mind what the immediate outcome is. Saleh Tyabji asks me to send you to Burma and Andrews thinks of you in connection with S.A. As for Ceylon the idea of a Congress deputation came to me spontaneously, not so these two even after the promptings. But of these when we meet. I hope you are fresh and that Krishna is enjoying herself.

Love,
Bapu

4

This letter was originally written in Hindi.

Poona,
13 November, 1945

My Dear Jawaharlal,

Our talk of yesterday's made me glad. I am sorry it could not be longer. I feel it cannot be finished in a single sitting, but will necessitate frequent meetings between us. I am so constituted that, if only I were physically fit to run about, I would myself overtake you, wherever you might be, and return after a couple of days' heart-to-heart talk with you. I have done so before. It is necessary that we understand each other well and that others also should clearly understand where we stand. It would not matter if ultimately we might have to agree to differ so long as we remained one at heart as we are today. The impression that I have gathered from our yesterday's talk is that there is not much difference in our outlook. To test this I put down below the gist of what I have understood. Please correct me if there is any discrepancy.

The real question, according to you, is how to bring about man's highest intellectual, economic, political and moral development. I agree entirely.

In this there should be an equal right and opportunity for all.

In other words, there should be equality between the town-dwellers and the villagers in the standard of food and drink, clothing and other living conditions. In order to achieve this equality today people should be able to produce for themselves the necessaries of life, i.e. clothing, food-stuffs, dwelling and lighting and water.

Man is not born to live in isolation but is essentially a social animal independent and interdependent. No one can or should ride on another's back. If we try to work out the necessary conditions for such a life, we are forced to the conclusion that the unit of society should be a village, or call it a small and manageable group of people who would, in the ideal, be self-sufficient (in the matter of their vital requirements) as a unit and bound together in bonds of mutual co-operation and inter-dependence.

If I find that so far I have understood you correctly, I shall take up consideration of the second part of the question in my next. I had got Rajkumari to translate into English my first letter to you. It is still lying with me. I am enclosing for you an English translation of this. It will serve a double purpose. An English translation might enable me to explain myself more fully and clearly to you. Further, it will enable me to find out precisely if I have fully and correctly understood you. Blessings for Indu.

Blessings from,
Bapu

5

My Dear Bapu,

I have received today, on return from Lucknow, your letter of the 5th October. I am glad you have written to me fully and I shall try to reply at some length but I hope you will forgive me if there is some delay in this, as I am at present tied up with close-fitting engagements. I am only here now for a day and a half. It is really better to have informal talks but just at present I do not know when to fit this in. I shall try.

Briefly put, my view is that the question before us is not one of truth versus untruth or non-violence versus violence. One assumes as one must that true co-operation and peaceful methods must be aimed at and a society which encourages these must be our objective. The whole question is how to achieve this society and what its content should be. I do not understand why a village should necessarily embody truth and non-violence. A village, normally speaking, is backward intellectually and culturally and no progress can be made from a backward environment. Narrow-minded people are much more likely to be untruthful and violent.

Then again we have to put down certain objectives like a sufficiency of food, clothing, housing, education, sanitation, etc. which should be the minimum requirements for the country and for everyone. It is with these objectives in view that we must find out specifically how to attain them speedily. Again it seems to me inevitable that modern means of transport as well as many other modern developments must continue and

69

be developed. There is no way out of it except to have them. If that is so inevitably a measure of heavy industry exists. How far that will fit in with a purely village society? Personally I hope that heavy or light industries should all be decentralized as far as possible and this is feasible now because of the development of electric power. If two types of economy exist in the country there should be either conflict between the two or one will overwhelm the other.

The question of independence and protection from foreign aggression, both political and economic, has also to be considered in this context. I do not think it is possible for India to be really independent unless she is a technically advanced country. I am not thinking for the moment in terms of just armies but rather of scientific growth. In the present context of the world we cannot even advance culturally without a strong-background of scientific research in every department. There is today in the world a tremendous acquisitive tendency both in individuals and groups and nations, which leads to conflicts and wars. Our entire society is based on this more or less. That basis must go and be transformed into one of co-operation, not of isolation which is impossible. If this is admitted and is found feasible then attempts should be made to realize it not in terms of an economy, which is cut off from the rest of the world, but rather one which co-operates. From the economic or political point of view an isolated India may well be a kind of vacuum which increases the acquisitive tendencies of others and thus creates conflicts.

There is no question of palaces for millions of people. But there seems to be no reason why millions should not have comfortable up-to-date homes where they can lead a cultured existence. Many of the present overgrown cities have developed evils which are deplorable. Probably we have to discourage this overgrowth and at the same time encourage the village to approximate more to the culture of the town.

It is many years ago since I read *Hind Swaraj* and I have only a vague picture in my mind. But even when I read it twenty or more years ago it seemed to me completely unreal. In your writings and speeches since then I have found much that seemed to me an advance on that old position and an appreciation of modern trends. I was therefore surprised when you told us that the old picture still remains intact in your mind. As you know, the Congress has never considered that picture, much less adopted it. You yourself have never asked it to adopt it except for certain relatively minor aspects of it. How far it is desirable for the Congress to consider these fundamental questions, involving varying philosophies of life, it is for you to judge. I should imagine that a body like the Congress should not lose itself in arguments over such matters which can only produce great confusion in people's minds resulting in inability to act in the present. This may also result in creating barriers between the Congress and others in the country. Ultimately of course this and other questions will have to be decided by representatives of free India. I have a feeling that most of these questions are thought of and discussed in terms of long ago, ignoring the vast changes that have taken place all over the world during the last generation or more. It is thirty-eight years since *Hind Swaraj* was written. The world has completely changed since then, possibly in a wrong direction. In any event any consideration of these questions must keep present facts, forces and the human material we have today in view, otherwise it will be divorced from reality. You are right in saying that the world, or a large part of it, appears to be bent on committing suicide. That may be an inevitable development of an evil seed in civilization that has grown. I think it is so. How to get rid of this evil, and yet how to keep the good in the present as in the past is our problem. Obviously there is good too in the present.

These are some random thoughts hurriedly written down and I fear they do injustice to the grave import of the questions raised. You will forgive me, I hope, for this jumbled presentation. Later I shall try to write more clearly on the subject.

About Hindustani Prachar Sabha and about Kasturba Fund, it is obvious that both of them have my sympathy and I think they are doing good work. But I am not quite sure about the manner of their working and I have a feeling that this is not always to my liking. I really do not know enough about them to be definite. But at present I have developed distaste for adding to my burden of responsibilities when I feel that I cannot probably undertake them for lack of time. These next few months and more are likely to be fevered ones for me and others. It seems hardly desirable to me, therefore, to join any responsible committee for form's sake only.

About Sarat Bose, I am completely in the dark; as to why he should grow so angry with me, unless it is some past grievance about my general attitude in regard to foreign relations. Whether I was right or wrong it does seem to me that Sarat has acted in a childish and irresponsible manner. You will remember perhaps that Subhash did not favour in the old days the Congress attitude towards Spain, Czechoslovakia, Munich and China. Perhaps this is a reflection of that old divergence of views. I know of nothing else that has happened.

I see that you are going to Bengal early in November.

Perhaps I may visit Calcutta for three or four days just then. If so, I hope to meet you.

You may have seen in the papers an invitation by the President of the newly formed Indonesian Republic to me and some others to visit Java. In view of the special circumstances of the case I decided immediately to accept this invitation subject of course to my getting the necessary facilities for going there. It is extremely doubtful if I shall get the facilities, and so probably I shall not go. Java is just two days by air from India, or even one day from Calcutta. The Vice-President of this Indonesian Republic, Mohammad Hatta, is a very old friend of mine. I suppose you know that the Javanese population is almost entirely Muslim.

I hope you are keeping well and have completely recovered from the attack of influenza.

Yours affectionately,
Jawaharlal

B.G. Tilak

Bal Gangadhar Tilak (1856–1920), part of the famous 'Lal Bal Pal' trio, was a nationalist and freedom fighter who remains revered to this day as 'Lokamanya' Tilak. He was one of the earliest advocates of Swaraj, or self-rule, and is famous for the saying, 'Swarajya is my birthright and I shall have it!' His correspondence with Gandhiji sheds light on the contrasting currents of a fascinating period in the freedom struggle, and the development of many subsequent movements.

1

This letter was in response to Tilak's proposal of publishing a prior interview between Gandhiji and him. These were still early years, with Gandhiji yet to achieve the foothold he would eventually have in India; as such, he wanted to avoid controversy.

Ahmedabad,
27 July, 1915

Dear Mr Tilak,

I have your note. I have not given anyone any authority to use my name in connection with the interviews I had with you. I have not even read the things you are referring to. The conversations between us were private and must remain so. The draft sent by you hardly does justice to the interview. I never said that I spoke for the Congress party or with its authority. I simply came as a friend and admirer and for friends. I did not know what view the Congress party would take. I simply put a tentative proposal before you.

I hope you will respect my wish not to be drawn in a newspaper controversy and that you will in no case publish the interview.

I am,

Yours sincerely,
M.K. GANDHI

2

Gandhiji wrote this letter to Tilak explaining how his position was different from that of both extremists and moderates. It was originally written in Hindi.

25 August,
1918

I have your letter. I am grateful to you for your sympathy. How can you not be concerned about my health? God be thanked I am now well. Of course I shall not be able to leave my bed for a few days. There was great pain. It has only now subsided. I do not propose to attend the Congress or the Moderates' Conference either. I see that my views are different from those of either. I have already told you about them. My view is that if all of us take up the work of recruitment for the war and enlist hundreds of thousands of recruits we can render a very great service to India. I know that Mrs Besant and you do not share this view. The Moderates also will not take up the work earnestly. This is one thing. My other point is that we accept the substance of the Montagu-Chelmsford Scheme, explain clearly the improvements that we wish to be made in it and fight till death to have these improvements accepted. That the Moderates will not accept this is clear enough. Even if Mrs Besant and you accept it, you will certainly not fight in the way I wish to fight. Mrs Besant has declared that she is not a Satyagrahi. You recognize satyagraha as [only] a weapon of the weak. I do not wish to get caught in this false position. And I do not wish to carry on an agitation in the Congress in opposition to you both. I have unshakable faith in my own formula. And it is my conviction that if my tapasya is complete, both Mrs. Besant and you will accept my formula. I can be patient. That the Moderates and the Extremists should each abandon some minor positions and come together is a thing repugnant to me. There are two wings in the country. I do not believe that it will do any harm to make the positions of both clear to the Government and the people. I do not at all like the attempt to bring together the Extremists and the Moderates. It will do much good if both the parties boldly proclaim their respective positions before the Government and the people. May God help you in your undertaking.

Yours,
Mohandas

3

This letter was in response to Lokamanya Tilak's letter dated 18 January 1920, in which Tilak says:

> *I am sorry to see that in your article on 'Reforms Resolution' in the last issue, you have represented me as holding that I considered 'everything fair in politics.' I write this to you to say that my view is not correctly represented therein. Politics is a game of worldly people and not of sadhus, and instead of the maxim as preached by Buddha, I prefer to rely on the maxim of Shri Krishna. That explains the whole difference and also the meaning of my phrase 'responsive co-operation.' Both methods are equally honest and righteous but the one is more suited to this world than the other. Any further explanation about the difference will be found in my* Gita Rahasya.

Delhi,
[28 January, 1920]

I naturally feel the greatest diffidence about joining issue with the Lokamanya in matters involving questions of interpretation of religious work. But there are things in or about which instinct transcends even interpretation. For me there is no conflict between the two texts quoted by the Lokamanya. The Buddhist text lays down an eternal principle. The text from the Bhagavad Gita shows to me how the principle of conquering hate by love, untruth by truth, can and must be applied. If it be true that God metes out the same measure to us that we mete out to others, it follows that if we would escape condign punishment, we may not return anger but gentleness even against anger. And this is the law not for the unworldly but essentially for the worldly. With deference to the Lokamanya, I venture to say that it betrays mental laziness to think that the world is not for sadhus. The epitome of all religions is to promote purushartha, and purushartha is nothing but a desperate attempt to become sadhu, i.e., to become a gentleman in every sense of the term. Finally, when I wrote the sentence about 'everything being fair in politics' according to the Lokamanya's creed, I had in mind his oft-repeated quotation. To me it enunciates bad law. And I shall not despair of the Lokamanya with all his acumen agreeably surprising India one day with a philosophical dissertation proving the falsity of the doctrine. In any case I pit the experience of a third of a century against the doctrine underlying 'evil unto evil'. The true law is 'truth even unto evil'.

M.K. Gandhi
Young India,
28–1–1920

4

Tribute to Tilak

This short message was published in The Bombay Chronicle *as a eulogy after Tilak's death.*

2 August, 1920

Love of India was the breath of life with Mr Tilak and in it he has left to us a treasure, which can only increase, by use. The endless procession of yesterday shows the hold the great patriot had on the masses.

M.K. Gandhi
The Bombay Chronicle,
3–8–1920

5

Lokamanya Tilak: An Obituary

This obituary appeared on the first page of Young India *on 4 August 1920.*

Lokamanya Bal Gangadhar Tilak is no more. It is difficult to believe of him as dead. He was so much part of the people. No man of our times had the hold on the masses that Mr Tilak had. The devotion that he commanded from thousands of his countrymen was extraordinary. He was unquestionably the idol of his people. His word was law among thousands. A giant among men has fallen. The voice of the lion is hushed. What was the reason for his hold upon his countrymen? I think the answer is simple. His patriotism was a passion with him. He knew no religion but love of his country. He was a born democrat. He believed in the rule of majority with an intensity that fairly frightened me. But that gave him his hold. He had an iron will, which he used for his country. His life was an open book. His tastes were simple. His private life was spotlessly clean. He had dedicated his wonderful talents to his country. No man preached the gospel of swaraj with the consistency and the insistence of Lokamanya. His countrymen therefore implicitly believed in him. His courage never failed him. His optimism was irrepressible. He had hoped to see swaraj fully established during his lifetime. If he failed, it was not his fault. He certainly brought it nearer by many a year. It is for us, who remain behind, to put forth redoubled effort to make it a reality in the shortest possible time. Lokamanya was an implacable foe of the bureaucracy, but this is not to say that he was a hater of Englishmen or English rule. I warn Englishmen against making the mistake of thinking that he was their enemy. I had the privilege of listening to an impromptu, learned discourse by him, at the time of the last Calcutta Congress, on Hindi being the national language. He had just returned from the Congress pandal. It was a treat to listen to his calm discourse on Hindi. In the course of his address he paid a glowing tribute to the English for their care of the vernaculars. His English visit, in spite of his sad experience of English juries, made him a staunch believer in British democracy and he even seriously made the amazing suggestion that India should instruct it on the Punjab through the cinematograph. I relate this incident not because I share his belief (for I do not), but in order to show that he entertained no hatred for Englishmen. But he could not and would not put up with an inferior status for India in the Empire. He wanted immediate equality, which he believed was his country's birthright. And in his struggle for India's freedom he did not spare the Government. In the battle for freedom he gave no quarter and asked for none. I hope that Englishmen will recognize the worth of the man whom India has adored. For us, he will go down to the generations yet unborn as a maker of modern India. They will revere his memory as of a man who lived for them and died for them. It is blasphemy to talk of such a man as dead. The permanent essence of him abides with us forever. Let us erect for the only Lokamanya of India an imperishable monument by weaving into our own lives his bravery, his simplicity, his wonderful industry and his love of his country. May God grant his soul peace.

Young India,
4–8–1920

Miraben

Miss Madeleine Slade (1892–1982), fondly known as Miraben, was the daughter of admiral Sir Edmond Slade. She came into contact with Gandhiji through the works of Romain Rolland and left Europe to meet him. She started living in Sabarmati Ashram in November 1925, and became Gandhiji's accomplice.

1

63, Bedford Gardens,
Campden Hill,
London, W. 8, Paris,
29 May, 1925

Most Dear Master,

I thank you profoundly for having answered my first letter to you—I had never dared to hope such a thing! I have eagerly taken to heart all you said, and I now venture to write to you again, my year of self-imposed trial being more than half over.

The first impulse has never faded, but on the contrary my desire to serve you has grown ever more and more fervent. It is impossible to express in words the greatness of the inspiration which impels me but I pray God with all my heart that I may be able to give expression to my love in work—in acts. However humble they may be they will at least be utterly sincere.

And now I want to put before you my most earnest request:

May I come to your Ashram to study spinning and weaving, to learn to live your ideals and principles in daily life, and indeed to learn in what way I may hope to serve you in the future? In order to become a fit servant of your cause I feel the absolute necessity of that training and I will do my very best to be a not too unworthy pupil if you will accept me!

In the meantime I continue my preparations as best I can. I spin and weave (only with wool, nobody seeming to know about the management of cotton in France or England). With the aid of many kind Indian friends I perplex my head over long Hindustani exercises I read. What a revelation is that reading! The more I enter into Indian thought, the more I feel as if I were reaching at last, a long lost home.

In matters of daily life I simplify as much as is possible under present circumstances. I have given up the drinking of all wines, beers or spirits, and I no longer eat meat of any kind.

My being is filled with a great joy and a great anguish. The joy of giving all I have to you and to your people and the anguish of being able to give so little.

I pine for the day when I shall come to India. Alas, there are still five months to wait! I reach Bombay on November 6th, and if I am permitted to join the Ashram I will take the train that evening arriving at Ahmedabad the next morning.

Dear Master, may I come?

Please do not think of troubling to reply to this letter yourself, but perhaps you could send me a word of answer through someone else.

Ever your humble and most devoted servant,

Madeleine Slade

PS. Enclosed are two little samples of wool which I have spun.

2

148, Russa Road,
Calcutta,
24 July, 1925

Dear Friend,

I was pleased to receive your letter which has touched me deeply. The samples of wool you have sent are excellent.

You are welcome whenever you choose to come. If I have advice of the steamer that brings you, there will be someone receiving you at the steamer, and guiding you to the train that will take you to Sabarmati. Only please remember that the life at the Ashram is not all rosy. It is strenuous. Bodily labour is given by every inmate. The climate of this country is also not a small consideration. I mention these things not to frighten you, but merely to warn you.

Yours sincerely,
M.K. Gandhi

PS. As my right hand requires rest, I am dictating my correspondence.

Romain Rolland

Romain Rolland (1866–1944) was a noted French writer, thinker and pacifist, who became a close associate of Gandhiji. Rolland won the Nobel Prize in 1915, becoming the first Nobel Laureate in Literature after Tagore in 1913.

1

Dear Friend,

I received your kind letter. Miss Slade arrived a little later. What a treasure you have sent me. I shall try to be worthy of such a great confidence. I shall do everything to help Miss Slade to become a little bridge between West and East. I am too imperfect to have a disciple. She will be my companion in my research (for truth) and as I am older and consequently more advanced in spiritual experience, I propose to share with you the honour of your paternity. Miss Slade shows a marvellous capacity for adaptation and we are already quite at ease with her. I leave Miss Slade to tell you the rest by asking her to speak to you of a French sister who has arrived at the Ashram just a few days before her.

2

Dear Friend,

Mira has translated your latest letter for me. My whole soul
goes out to you in your grief especially because it comes over
a letter which makes you suspect me of hardness of heart. I
appreciate your desire to find me correct in all I do and think.
I do indeed want to stand well with you, but I must be true
to myself if I am to continue to deserve your warm friendship.

Let me first tell you that Mira's letter reflected her own
views though they were found to coincide with mine. Neither
Mira, so far as I know her, nor I had the remotest idea of
judging those two good peasants. Their action was undoubtedly
one of heroism. What we had in our minds was the heroism
of a war resister, and from the record sent by you and as it
was interpreted to me by Mira, I missed that particular type
of heroism which a war resister demonstrates in his own life.
Joan of Arc was a heroine. So were Leonidas and Horatius.
But the heroism in each case was of a different type, each
noble and admirable in its sphere.

In the answers given by the peasants, I do not notice
any definite repugnance to war as war and a determination
to suffer to the uttermost in their resistance to war. These
peasant friends, if my recollection serves me right, are heroes
representing and defending the simple rustic life. These heroes
are no less precious than those of a militant war resister type.
We want to treasure all this heroism, but what I feel is that

we will serve the heroes and the cause of truth better if we treated each type separately.

You have curiously raised the question of my participation in the late War. It is a legitimate question. I had answered it in the last autobiographical chapter as if in anticipation of your question. Please read it carefully and tell me at your leisure what you think of the argument. I shall treasure your opinion.

Lastly, I do want to reach perfection, but I recognize my limitations, and the recognition is becoming clearer day after day. Who knows in how many places I must be guilty of hardness of heart, and I should not be surprised if you have noticed want of charity in my writings in more places than one. I can only tell you that the lapses are there in spite of my prayerful effort to the contrary. I suppose it was not without reason that the early Christians considered Satan to be not merely an evil principle but evil incarnate. He seems to dominate us in every walk of life and man's mission is to overthrow him from power.

This letter of yours to Mira makes me more and more anxious to see you in the flesh, and there is just a distant hope of my being able to do so this year if I keep good health and if otherwise the inner voice guides me towards Europe. I am seriously considering two invitations, and the desire to meet you may precipitate my decision in favour of accepting those invitations.

Yours sincerely,
M.K. Gandhi

M.A. Jinnah

Muhammad Ali Jinnah (1876–1948) was the founder of Pakistan, and its first Governor-General. The Partition of the Indian subcontinent is now infamous in the annals of history, both for the massive loss of life and property that it caused, and for the birth of the twin nations of India and Pakistan. The following correspondence, between two of the key figures involved in the event (albeit on opposite sides), is a significant record of the debates, actions, social context and thought processes that led up to it in a few years.

1

Dear Mr Jinnah,

Pandit Nehru told me yesterday that you were complaining to Maulana Sahib about the absence of any reply from me to your letter of the 5th November in reply to mine of the 19th October. The letter was received by me when I was pronounced by the Doctors to be seriously ill at Calcutta.

The letter was shown to me three days after its receipt. Had I thought it necessarily called for a reply even though I was ill I would have sent one. I read the letter and I still think there was nothing useful that I could have said in reply. But in a way I am glad you awaited a reply and here it is. Mr Kher told me definitely he had a private message from you. He delivered it to me when I was alone. I could have sent you a verbal message in reply but in order to give you a true picture of my mental state I sent you a short note. There was nothing to hide in it. But I did feel, as I still do, that the way in which you used it came upon me as a painful surprise.

Your complain of my silence. The reason for my silence is literally and truly in my note. Believe me, the moment I can do something that can bring the two communities together nothing in the world can prevent me from so doing. You seem to deny that your speech was declaration of war, but your later pronouncements too confirmed my first impression. How can I prove what is a matter of feeling? In your speech I miss the old Nationalist when in 1915 I returned from my self-imposed exile in South Africa. Everybody spoke of you as one of the staunchest nationalists and the hope of both the Hindus and Mussalmans. Are you still the same Mr Jinnah?

If you say you are, in spite of your speeches, I shall accept your word.

Lastly, you want me to come forward with some proposal. What proposal can I make except to ask you on bended knees to be what I thought you were? But the proposals to form the basis of unity between the two communities surely have got to come from you.

This again is not for publication but for your eyes; it is the one of a friend, not of an opponent.

Yours sincerely,
M.K. Gandhi

2

22 September, 1944

Dear Quaid-I-Azam,

Your letter of yesterday so disturbed me that I thought I would postpone my reply till after we had met at the usual time. Though I made no advance at our meeting, I think I see somewhat clearly what you are driving at. The more I think about the two nations theory the more alarming it appears to be. The book recommended by you gives me no help. It contains half-truths and its conclusions or inferences are unwarranted. I am unable to accept the proposition that the Muslims of India are a nation distinct from the rest of the inhabitants of India. Mere assertion is no proof. The consequences of accepting such a proposition are dangerous in the extreme. Once the principle is admitted there would be no limit to claims for cutting up India into numerous divisions which would spell India's ruin. I have therefore suggested a way out. Let it be a partition as between two brothers, if a division there must be.

You seem to be averse to a plebiscite. In spite of the admitted importance of the League, there must be clear proof that the people affected desire partition. In my opinion, all the people inhabiting the area ought to express their opinion specifically on this single issue of division. Adult suffrage is the best method, but I would accept any other equivalent.

You summarily reject the idea of common interest between the two arms. I can be no willing party to a division which does not provide for the simultaneous safeguarding of common interests such as defence, foreign affairs and the like. There will be no feeling of security by the people of India without a recognition of the natural and mutual obligations arising out of physical contiguity.

Your letter shows a wide divergence of opinion and outlook between us. Thus you adhere to the opinion often expressed by you that the August 1942 resolution is 'inimical to the ideals and demands of Muslim India'. There is no proof for this sweeping statement.

We seem to be moving in a circle. I have made a suggestion. If we are bent on agreeing, as I hope we are, let us call in a third party or parties to guide or even arbitrate between us.

Yours sincerely,
M.K. Gandhi

3

Dear Quaid-I-Azam,

Last evening's talk has left a bad taste in the mouth. Our talks and our correspondence seem to run in parallel lines and never touch one another. We reached the breaking point last evening but, thank God, we were unwilling to part. We resumed discussion and suspended it in order to allow me to keep my time for the evening public prayer.

In order that all possible chance of making any mistake in a matter of this great importance may be removed, I would like you to give me in writing what precisely on your part you would want me to put my signature to.

I adhere to my suggestion that we may call in some outside assistance to help us at this stage.

Yours sincerely,
M.K. Gandhi

4

Dear Mr Gandhi,

I am in receipt of your letter of September 23. May I refer you to my letter to today's date which I sent to you in reply to yours of September 22? I have nothing new or fresh to add, but I may say that it is not a case of your being asked to put your signature as representing anybody till you clothe yourself with representing capacity and are vested with authority. We stand by, as I have already said, the basic and fundamental principles embodied in the Lahore resolution of March 1940. I appeal to you once more to revise your policy and programme, as the future of this subcontinent and the welfare of the peoples of India demand that you should face realities.

Yours sincerely,
M.A. Jinnah

5

Dear Qaid-I-Azam,

I have your two letters of September 23 in reply to my letters of the 22nd and 23rd.

With your assistance, I am exploring the possibilities of reaching an agreement, so that the claim embodied in the Muslim League resolution of Lahore may be reasonably satisfied. You must therefore have no apprehensions that the August resolution will stand in the way of our reaching an agreement. That resolution dealt with the question of India as against Britain and it cannot stand in the way of our settlement.

I proceed on the assumption that India is not to be regarded as two or more nations but as one family consisting of many members of whom the Muslims living in the north-west zones, i.e. Baluchistan, Sind, North-West Frontier Province and that part of the Punjab where they are in absolute majority over all the other elements and in parts of Bengal and Assam where they are in absolute majority, desire to live in separation from the rest of India.

Differing from you on the general basis, I can yet recommend to the Congress and the country the acceptance of the claim for separation contained in the Muslim League resolution of Lahore of 1940, on my basis and on the following terms:

The areas should be demarcated by a Commission approved by the Congress and the League. The wishes of the inhabitants of the areas demarcated should be ascertained through the votes of the adult population of the areas or through some equivalent method.

If the vote is in favour of separation it shall be agreed that these areas shall form a separate State as soon as possible after India is free from foreign domination and can therefore be constituted into two sovereign independent States.

There shall be a treaty of separation which should also provide for the efficient and satisfactory administration of foreign affairs, defence, internal communications, customs, commerce and the like, which must necessarily continue to be matters of common interest between the contracting parties.

The treaty shall also contain terms for safeguarding the rights of minorities in the two States.

Immediately on the acceptance of this agreement by the Congress and the League the two shall decide upon a common course of action for the attainment of independence of India.

The League will however be free to remain out of any direct action to which the Congress may resort and in which the League may not be willing to participate.

If you do not agree to these terms, could you let me know in precise terms what you would have me to accept in terms of the Lahore resolution and bind myself to recommend to the Congress? If you could kindly do this, I shall be able to see, apart from the difference in approach, what definite terms I can agree to. In your letter of September 23, you refer to 'the basic and fundamental principles embodied in the Lahore resolution' and ask me to accept them.

Surely this is unnecessary when, as I feel, I have accepted the concrete consequence that should follow from such acceptance.

Yours sincerely,
M.K. Gandhi

Adolf Hitler

As the whole world hurtled towards War, Gandhiji wrote two letters to Adolf Hitler (1889–1945), taking it upon himself to appeal to the better senses of the Nazi leader and prevent a global conflict of unprecedented scale. Addressing the Führer as 'friend', Gandhiji made an earnest effort to find common ground with him through their love for their respective nations and their opposition to British imperialism, while denouncing his genocidal and aggressive actions. As later events show, in this, Gandhiji was not successful.

1

As at Wardha, C.P., INDIA,
23 July, 1939

Dear Friend,

Friends have been urging me to write to you for the sake of humanity. But I have resisted their request, because of the feeling that any letter from me would be impertinence. Something tells me that I must not calculate and that I must make my appeal for whatever it may be worth.

It is quite clear that you are today the one person in the world who can prevent a war which may reduce humanity to a savage state. Must you pay that price for an object however worthy it may appear to you to be? Will you listen to the appeal of one who has deliberately shunned the method of war not without considerable success? Any way I anticipate your forgiveness, if I have erred in writing to you.

I remain,

Your sincere friend,
M.K. Gandhi

2

Dear Friend,

That I address you as a friend is no formality. I own no foes. My business in life has been for the past thirty-three years to enlist the friendship of the whole of humanity by befriending mankind, irrespective of race, colour or creed.

I hope you will have the time and desire to know how a good portion of humanity who have been living under the influence of that doctrine of universal friendship view your action. We have no doubt about your bravery or devotion to your fatherland, nor do we believe that you are the monster described by your opponents. But your own writings and pronouncements and those of your friends and admirers leave no room for doubt that many of your acts are monstrous and unbecoming of human dignity, especially in the estimation of men like me who believe in universal friendliness. Such are your humiliation of Czechoslovakia, the rape of Poland and the swallowing of Denmark. I am aware that your view of life regards such spoliations as virtuous acts. But we have been taught from childhood to regard them as acts degrading humanity. Hence we cannot possibly wish success to your arms.

But ours is a unique position. We resist British Imperialism no less than Nazism. If there is a difference, it is in degree. One-fifth of the human race has been brought under the British heel by means that will not bear scrutiny. Our resistance to it does not mean harm to the British people. We seek to convert them, not to defeat them on the battlefield. Ours is an unarmed revolt against the British rule. But whether we convert them or not, we are determined to make their rule impossible by non-violent non-co-operation. It is a method in its nature indefensible. It is based on the knowledge that no spoliator can compass his end without a certain degree of co-operation, willing or compulsory, of the victim. Our rulers may have our land and bodies but not our souls. They can have the former only by complete destruction of every Indian—man, woman and child. That all may not rise to that degree of heroism and that a fair amount of frightfulness can bend the back of revolt is true but the argument would be beside the point. For, if a fair number of men and women be found in India who would be prepared without any ill will against the spoliators to lay down their lives rather than bend the knee to them, they would have shown the way to freedom from the tyranny of violence. I ask you to believe me when I say that you will find an unexpected number of such men and women in India. They have been having that training for the past twenty years.

We have been trying for the past half a century to throw off the British rule. The movement of independence has been never so strong as now. The most powerful political organization, I mean the Indian National Congress, is trying to achieve this end. We have attained a very fair measure of success through non-violent effort. We were groping for the right means to combat the most organized violence in the world which the British power represents. You have challenged it. It remains to be seen which is the better organized, the German or the British. We know what the British heel means for us and the non-European races of the world. But we would never wish to end the British rule with German aid. We have found in non-violence a force which, if organized, can without doubt match itself against a combination of all the most violent forces in the world. In non-violent technique, as I have said, there is no such thing as defeat. It is all 'do or die' without killing or hurting. It can be used practically without money and obviously without the aid of science of destruction which you have brought to such perfection. It is a marvel to me that you do not see that it is nobody's monopoly. If not the British, some other power will certainly improve upon your method and beat you with your own weapon. You are leaving no legacy to your people of which they would feel proud. They cannot take pride in a recital of cruel deed, however skilfully planned. I, therefore, appeal to you in the name of humanity to stop the war. You will lose nothing by referring all the matters of dispute between you and Great Britain to an international tribunal of your joint choice. If you attain success in the war, it will not prove that you were in the right. It will only prove that your power of destruction was greater. Whereas an award by an impartial tribunal will show as far as it is humanly possible which party was in the right.

You know that not long ago I made an appeal to every Briton to accept my method of non-violent resistance. I did it because the British know me as a friend though a rebel. I am a stranger to you and your people. I have not the courage to make you the appeal I made to every Briton. Not that it would not apply to you with the same force as to the British. But my present proposal is much simple because much more practical and familiar.

During this season when the hearts of the peoples of Europe yearn for peace, we have suspended even our own peaceful struggle. Is it too much to ask you to make an effort for peace during a time which may mean nothing to you personally but which must mean much to the millions of Europeans whose dumb cry for peace I hear, for my ears are attended to hearing the dumb millions? I had intended to address a joint appeal to you and Signor Mussolini, whom I had the privilege of meeting when I was in Rome during my visit to England as a delegate to the Round Table Conference. I hope that he will take this as addressed to him also with the necessary changes.

I am,

Your sincere friend,
M.K. Gandhi

C. Rajagopalachari

C. Rajagopalachari (1879–1972) was a lawyer, journalist, author and statesman, who became the second (and last) Governor-General of Independent India (1948–50).

1

My Dear Rajagopalachari,

Mahadev has shown me your letter to him. You must not despond. For Mrs Naidu to say that I am despondent is a libel. It is true that I am groping. There are things about which I give no clear-cut decisions. But that is to admit that we are voyaging in uncertain waters.

Remember we are Satyagrahis. Let me apply to the situation the law of the family. Assume that two brothers are quarrelling over the inheritance. Both want to use it for the good of the family. One at least knows he does not need it to serve the family. The majority of the clan would have him to cling to the inheritance. But is it not the duty of the Satyagrahi brother to forgo the inheritance and avoid a quarrel and consequent waste of time and energy? Is the case any different here? However, I am acting cautiously. All I am trying to do is to avoid an unseemly wrangle. I will take up the Presidentship, if I find that it will serve the country. There is plenty of time to decide. The returns of spinning are proving most instructive. Is it much use my presiding if the returns remain as poor as they are? Will it not then be better to retire from the Congress and have a rigid programme and a membership that is honest and willing? Is it any use having a vote for the wheel from persons clad in foreign stuff? And think of the exploitation of the simple folk for capturing the Congress! Will the so-called No-changers remain strictly honest? Picture to yourself the whole working. If we cannot retain the Congress without this tug of war, we must willingly surrender it. I have thought deeply over your letters but feel sure that I must retire from any such contest. But for the present I am simply watching. Am waiting for Motilalji's answer.

Now for Malabar. I have applications from many sources. What would you have me to do? I was thinking of sending someone to make special report in collaboration with you. But as nothing has yet been done I would like your suggestions. Plenty of clothing has been collected. Please guide me about its disposal too.

I have not been able to make much headway in Delhi. There is still some prospect of a settlement. But the thing is very delicate.

Yes, your guess is correct. The fair friend is Sarladevi. She wants to bombard me with more stuff but I have refused to give further accommodation. There are some beautiful letters from Brahmins in repudiation. I have published one.

Yours,
M.K.G.

2

My Dear C.R.,

Somehow or other I need your letter to feel that all is well with you. My position is this. My body and mind are living in a world by which I remain unaffected, but in which I am being tried. My soul is living in a world physically away from me and yet a world by which I am and want to be affected. You are a part of that world and perhaps the nearest to me. My innermost being wants your approbation of what I am doing and thinking. I may not always succeed in getting it, but it craves for your verdict.

Now you understand exactly why I want to hear from you apart from many other reasons. You must let me have if it is only a postcard every week. Mahadev, Devdas, Pyarelal should keep you posted with what is going on.

And you must keep well.

Your sadhana is the development of the place where you are and a scientific test of our theory of the value of hand-spinning. Even if it proves untrue in the end, neither we nor the world will have lost anything, for I know that we are true in the sense that we have full faith in the programme and, if it is intrinsically not immoral, our theory can be claimed to be true, when a fairly large number of villages sustain hand-spinning and Khadi without protection as the whole of India sustain home cookery without protection. Surely this is a long introduction to what I want to say. Here is Pitt's letter and the letters from Kelappan. I am simply saying that we must keep nominally a Satyagrahi at the Eastern gate unless the local men think otherwise. But you may come to other conclusion. You should write to Kelappan. He seems to be a nice, useful man.

With love,

Yours,
Bapu

Lord Irwin

A crucial moment in the history of India's freedom struggle, as well as Gandhi's personal history, was the Gandhi-Irwin Pact (1931) between Gandhiji and Lord Irwin (1881–1959), the then Viceroy of India (1926–1931). The Pact, born out of a vague promise made by Irwin of granting India 'dominion status' under the British Empire, while severely inadequate, was nevertheless a step towards India's eventual independence. The following letters provide important context for the Pact.

1

Satyagraha Ashram,
Sabarmati,
2 March, 1930

Dear Friend,

Before embarking on civil disobedience, and taking the risk I have dreaded to take all these years, I would fain approach you and find a way out.

My personal faith is absolutely clear. I cannot intentionally hurt anything that lives, much less fellow human beings, even though they may do the greatest wrong to me and mine. Whilst, therefore, I hold the British rule to be a curse, I do not intend any harm to a single Englishman, or to any legitimate interest, he may have in India.

I must not be misunderstood. Though I hold the British rule in India to be a curse, I do not, therefore, consider Englishmen in general, to be worse than any other people on earth. I have the privilege of claiming many Englishmen as dearest friends. Indeed much that I have learnt of the evil of the British rule is due to the writings of frank and courageous Englishmen, who have not hesitated to tell the unpalatable truth about that rule.

And why do I regard the British rule as a curse?

It has impoverished the dumb millions by a system of progressive exploitation, and by a ruinously expensive military and civil administration which the country can never afford.

It has reduced us politically to serfdom. It has sapped the foundations of our culture. And, by the policy of cruel disarmament, it has degraded us spiritually.

Lacking the inward strength, we have been reduced, by all but universal disarmament, to a state bordering on cowardly helplessness.

In common with many of my countrymen, I had hugged the fond hope that the proposed Round Table Conference might furnish a solution. But when you said plainly that you could not give any assurance that you or the British Cabinet would pledge yourselves to support a scheme of full dominion status, the Round Table Conference could not possibly furnish the solution for which vocal India is consciously, and the dumb millions are unconsciously, thirsting. Needless to say, there never was any question of Parliament's verdict being anticipated. Instances are not wanting of the British Cabinet, in anticipation of the parliamentary verdict, having itself pledged to a particular policy.

The Delhi interview having miscarried, there was no option for Pandit Motilal Nehru and me, but to take steps, to carry out the solemn resolution of the Congress arrived at in Calcutta at its session in 1928.

But the resolution of independence should cause no alarm, if the word dominion status mentioned in your announcement had been used in its accepted sense. For, has it not been admitted by the responsible British statesmen, that dominion status is virtual independence? What, however, I fear is that there never has been any intention of granting such dominion status to India, in the immediate future.

But this is past history. Since the announcement many events have happened which show unmistakably the trend of British policy.

It seems as clear as daylight that responsible British statesmen do not contemplate any alteration in British policy, that might adversely affect Britain's commerce with India, or require a close and impartial scrutiny of Britain's transactions with India. If nothing is done to end the process of exploitation, India must be bled with an ever increasing speed. The Finance Member regards as a settled fact the ratio which by a stroke of the pen drains India of a few crores. And when a serious attempt is being made through a civil form of direct action, to unsettle this fact, among many others, even you cannot help appealing to the wealthy landed classes, to help you to crush that attempt, in the name of an order that grinds India to atoms.

Unless those who work in the name of the nation understand and keep before all concerned, the motive that lies behind this craving for independence, there is every danger of independence itself coming to us so charged as to be of no value to those toiling voiceless millions, for whom it is sought, and for whom it is worth taking. It is for that reason, that I have been recently telling the public what independence should really mean.

Let me put before you some of the salient points.

The terrific pressure of land revenue, which furnishes a large part of the total, must undergo a considerable modification, in an independent India. Even the much vaunted permanent settlement benefits few rich zamindars, not the ryots. The ryot has remained as helpless as ever. He is a mere tenant at will. Not only, then, has land revenue to be considerably reduced, but the whole revenue system has to be so revised, as to make the ryot's good its primary concern. But the British system seems to be designed to crush the very life out of him. Even the salt he must use to live is so taxed as to make the burden fall heaviest on him, if only because of the heartless impartiality of its incidence. The tax shows itself more burdensome on the poor man; when it is remembered that salt is the one thing he must eat more than the rich, both individually and collectively. The drink and drug revenue, too, is derived from the poor. It saps the foundations both of their health and morals. It is defended under the false plea of individual freedom, but, in reality, is maintained for its own sake. The ingenuity of the authors of the reforms of 1919 transferred this revenue to the so-called responsible part of dyarchy, so as to throw the burden of prohibition on it, thus, from the very beginning, rendering it powerless for good. If the unhappy Minister wipes out this revenue he must starve education, since in the existing circumstances he has no new source of replacing that revenue. If the weight of taxation has crushed the poor from above, the destruction of the central supplementary industry, that is, hand-spinning, has undermined their capacity for producing wealth. The tale of India's ruination is not complete without reference to the liabilities incurred in her name. Sufficient has been recently said about these in the public press. It must be the duty of a free India to subject all the liabilities to the strictest investigation, and repudiate those that may be adjudged by an impartial tribunal to be unjust and unfair.

The iniquities sampled above are maintained in order to carry on a foreign administration, demonstrably the most expensive in the world. Take your own salary. It is over Rs 21,000 per month besides many other indirect additions. The British Prime Minister gets £5,000 per year, that is, Rs 5,400 per month, at the present rate of exchange. You are getting over Rs 700 per day, against India's average income of less than two annas per day. The Prime Minister gets Rs 180 per day, against Great Britain's average income of nearly Rs 2 per day. Thus you are getting much over five thousand times India's average income. The British Prime Minister is getting only ninety times Britain's average income. On bended knee I ask you to ponder over this phenomenon. I have taken a personal illustration to drive home a painful truth. I have too great a regard for you as a man to wish to hurt your feelings. I know that you do not need the salary you get. But a system that provides for such an arrangement deserves to be summarily scrapped. What is true of the Vice-Regal salary is true generally of the whole administration.

A radical cutting down of the revenue, therefore, depends upon an equally radical reduction in the expenses of the administration. This means a transformation of the scheme of government. This transformation is impossible without independence. And hence the spontaneous demonstration of 26th January, in which hundreds of thousands of villagers instinctively participated. To them independence means deliverance from the killing weight.

Not one of the great British political parties, it seems to me, is prepared to give up the Indian spoils to which Great Britain helps herself from day to day, often, in spite of the unanimous opposition of *Indian opinion.*

Nevertheless, if India is to live as a nation, if the slow death by starvation of her people is to stop, some remedy must be found for immediate relief. The proposed conference is certainly not the remedy. It is not a matter of carrying conviction by argument. The matter resolves itself into one of matching forces. Conviction or no conviction, Great Britain would defend her Indian commerce and interests by all the forces at her command. India must consequently evolve force enough to free herself from that embrace of death.

It is common cause that, however disorganized, and, for the time being, insignificant, it may be, the party of violence is gaining ground and making itself felt. Its end is the same as mine. But I am convinced that it cannot bring the desired relief to the dumb millions. The conviction is growing deeper and deeper in me that nothing but unadulterated non-violence can check the organized violence of the British Government. Many think that non-violence is not an active force. My experience, limited though it surely is, shows that non-violence can be an intensely active force. It is my purpose to set in motion that force as well against the organized violent force of the British rule, as the unorganized violent force of the growing party of violence. To sit still would be to give rein to both the forces above-mentioned. Having an unquestioning and immovable faith in the efficacy of non-violence, as I know it, it would be sinful on my part to wait any longer.

This non-violence will be expressed through civil disobedience, for the moment confined to the inmates of the Satyagraha Ashram, but ultimately designed to cover all those who choose to join the movement with its obvious limitations.

I know that in embarking on non-violence, I shall be running what might fairly be termed a mad risk. But the victories of truth have never been won without risks, often of the gravest character. Conversion of a nation that has consciously or unconsciously preyed upon another, far more numerous, far more ancient, and no less cultured than itself, is worth any amount of risk.

I have deliberately used the word conversion. For my ambition is no less than to convert the British people through non-violence, and thus to make them see the wrong they have done to India. I do not seek to harm your people. I want to serve them even as I want to serve my own. I believe that I have always served them.

I served them up to 1919, blindly. But when my eyes were opened and I conceived non-co-operation, the object still was to serve them. I employed the same weapon that I have, in all humility, successfully used against the dearest members of my family. If I have equal love for your people with mine, it will not long remain hidden. It will be acknowledged by them, even as the members of my family acknowledged, after they had tried me for several years. If the people join me, as I expect they will, the sufferings they will undergo, unless the British nation sooner retraces its steps, will be enough to melt the stoniest hearts.

The plan through civil disobedience will be to combat such evils as I have sampled out. If we want to sever the British connection it is because of such evils. When they are removed, the path becomes easy. Then the way to friendly negotiation will be open. If the British commerce with India is purified of greed, you will have no difficulty in recognizing our independence. I invite you then to pave the way for immediate removal of those evils, and thus open a way for a real conference between equals, interested only in promoting the common good of mankind through voluntary fellowship and in arranging terms of mutual help and commerce equally suited to both. You have unnecessarily laid stress upon communal problems that unhappily affect this land. Important though they undoubtedly are for the consideration of any scheme of Government they have little bearing on the greater problems which are above communities and which affect them all equally. But if you cannot see your way to deal with these evils and my letter makes no appeal to your heart, on the eleventh day of this month, I shall proceed with such co-workers of the Ashram as I can take, to disregard the provisions of the salt laws. I regard this tax to be the most iniquitous of all from the poor man's standpoint. As the independence movement is essentially for the poorest in the land, the beginning will be made with this evil. The wonder is that we have submitted to the cruel monopoly for so long. It is, I know, open to you to frustrate my design by arresting me. I hope that there will be tens of thousands ready, in a disciplined manner, to take up the work after me, and, in the act of disobeying the Salt Act, to lay themselves open to the penalties of a law that should never have disfigured the statute book.

I have no desire to cause you unnecessary embarrassment, or any at all, so far as I can help. If you think that there is any substance in my letter, and if you will care to discuss matters with me, and if to that end you would like me to postpone publication of this letter, I shall gladly refrain on receipt of a telegram to that effect soon after this reaches you. You will, however, do me the favour not to deflect me from my course, unless you can see your way to conform to the substance of this letter.

This letter is not in any way intended as a threat, but is a simple and sacred duty, peremptory on a civil resister. Therefore, I am having it specially delivered by a young English friend who believes in the Indian cause and is a full believer in non-violence and whom Providence seems to have sent to me, as it were, for the very purpose.

I remain,

Your sincere friend,
M.K. Gandhi

2

This letter was written by Gandhiji on the eve of his arrest on 4 May, 1930.

Dear Friend,

God willing, it is my intention... to set out for Dharasana and reach there with my companions... and demand possession of the Salt Works. The public have been told that Dharasana is a private property. This is mere camouflage. It is as effectively under Government control as the Viceroy's house. Not a pinch of salt can be removed without the previous sanction of the authorities.

It is possible for you to prevent this raid, as it has been playfully and mischievously called, in three ways:

By removing the Salt Tax;

By arresting me and my party, unless the country can, as I hope it will, replace every one taken away;

By sheer goondaism unless every head broken is replaced, as I hope it will.

It is not without hesitation that the step has been decided upon. I had hoped that the Government would fight the civil resisters in a civilized manner. I could have had nothing to say if, in dealing with the civil resisters, the Government has satisfied itself with applying the ordinary processes of law. Instead, whilst the known leaders have been dealt with more or less according to the legal formality, the rank and file has been often savagely and in some cases even indecently assaulted. Had there been isolated cases, they might have been overlooked. But accounts have come to me from Bengal, Bihar, Utkal, U.E, Delhi and Bombay confirming the experiences of Gujarat of which I have ample evidence at my disposal. In Karachi, Peshawar and Madras the firing would appear to have been unprovoked and unnecessary. Bones have been broken, private parts have been squeezed for the purpose of making volunteers give up, to the Government valueless, to the volunteers precious salt. At Muthra an Assistant Magistrate is said to have snatched the National Flag from a ten-year-old boy. The crowd demanding restoration of the Flag thus illegally seized is reported to have been mercilessly beaten back. That the Flag was subsequently restored betrayed a guilty conscience. In Bengal there seem to have been only a few prosecutions and assaults about salt, but unthinkable cruelties are said to have been practised in the act of snatching flags from volunteers. Paddy fields are reported to have been burnt, eatables forcibly taken. A vegetable market in Gujarat has been raided, because the dealers would not sell vegetables to officials. These acts have taken place in front of crowds who, for the sake of Congress mandate, have submitted without retaliation. I ask you to believe the accounts given by men pledged to truth. Repudiation even by high officials has, as in the Bardoli case, often proved false. The officials I regret to have to say, have not hesitated to publish falsehoods to the people even during the last five weeks. I take the following samples from Government notices issued from Collectors' offices in Gujarat:

'1. Adults use five pounds of salt per year, therefore pay three annas per year as tax. If Government removed the monopoly, people will have to pay higher prices and in addition make good to the Government the loss sustained by the removal of the monopoly. The salt you take from the sea-shore is not eatable, therefore the Government destroys it.'

'2. Mr Gandhi says that Government has destroyed hand-spinning in this country, whereas everybody knows that this is not true, because throughout the country there is not a village where hand-spinning of cotton is not going on. Moreover in every province cotton spinners are shown superior methods and are provided with better instruments at less prices and are thus helped by Government.'

'3. Out of every five rupees of the debt that the Government has incurred, rupees four have been beneficially spent.'

I have taken these three sets of statements from three different leaflets. I venture to suggest that everyone of these statements is demonstrably false. The daily consumption of salt by an adult is three times the amount stated and therefore the poll tax and the salt tax undoubtedly is at least 9 as. per head per year. And this tax is levied from man, woman, child and domestic cattle irrespective of age and health.

It is a wicked falsehood to say that every village has a spinning wheel and that the spinning movement is in any shape or form encouraged or supported by the Government. Financiers can better dispose of the falsehood that four out of every five rupees of the public debt is used for benefit of the public. But those falsehoods are mere samples of what people know is going on in every day contact with the Government. Only the other day a Gujarati poet, a brave man, was convicted on prejudged official evidence in spite of his emphatic statement that at the time mentioned he was sleeping soundly in another Place.

Now for instances of official inactivities. Liquor dealers have assaulted pickets admitted by officials to have been peaceful and sold liquor in contravention of regulations. The officials have taken no notice either of the assaults or the illegal sales of liquor. As to the assaults, though they are known to everybody, they may take shelter under the plea that they have received no complaints.

And now you have sprung upon the country a Press Ordinance surpassing any hitherto known in India. You have found a short cut through the law's delay in the matter of the trial of Bhagat Singh and others by doing away with the ordinary procedure. Is it any wonder if I call all these official activities and inactivities a veiled form of Martial Law? Yet this is only the fifth week of the struggle.

Before then the reign of terrorism that has just begun overwhelms India, I feel that I must take a bolder step and if possible divert your wrath in a cleaner if more drastic channel. You may not know the things that I have described. You may not even now believe in them. I can but invite your serious attention to them.

Anyway I feel that it would be cowardly on my part not to invite you to disclose to the full the leonine paws of authority, so that the people who are suffering tortures and destruction of their property may not feel that I, who had perhaps been the chief party inspiring them to action that has brought to right light the Government in its true colours, had left any stone unturned to work out the Satyagraha programme as fully as it was possible under given circumstances.

According to the science of Satyagraha, the greater the repression and lawlessness on the part of authority, the greater should be the suffering courted by the victims. Success is the certain result of suffering of the extremest character voluntarily undergone.

I know the dangers attendant upon the methods adopted by me. But the country is not likely to mistake my meaning. I say what I mean and think. And I have been saying for the last fifteen years in India, and outside for twenty years more, and repeat now that the only way to conquer violence is through non-violence pure and undefiled. I have said also that every violent act, word and even thought interferes with the progress of non-violent action. If in spite of such repeated warnings, people will resort to violence, I must own responsibility save such as inevitably attaches to every human being for the acts of every other human being. But the question of responsibility apart, I dare not postpone action on any cause whatsoever if non-violence is the force the seers of the world have claimed it to be and if I am not to belie my own extensive experience of its working.

But I would fain avoid the further steps. I would therefore ask you to remove the tax which many of your illustrious countrymen have condemned in unmeasured terms and which, as you could not have failed to observe, has evoked universal protest and resentment expressed in civil disobedience. You may condemn civil disobedience as much as you like. Will you prefer violent revolt to civil disobedience? If you say, as you have said, that the civil disobedience must end in violence, history will pronounce the verdict that the British Government not bearing because not understanding non-violence, goaded human nature to violence, which it could understand and deal with. But in spite of the goading, I shall hope that God will give the people of India wisdom and strength to withstand every temptation and provocation to violence.

If, therefore, you cannot see your way to remove the Salt Tax and remove the prohibitions on private salt-making I must reluctantly commence the march adumbrated in the opening paragraph of my letter.

I am,

Your sincere friend,
M.K. Gandhi

Lord Linlithgow

August 1942 saw serious political upheavals in the country in the form of 'Quit India' and 'Do or Die'. The government of the day launched a vicious propaganda campaign against Congress leaders and laid the entire responsibility for the August disturbance on them. The nationalists were unanimous in declaring that the crisis was precipitated by the repressive policy of the government. The entire country, from one end to the other, was aflame with unprecedented mob fury, and it appeared as if the Indian action had once and for all decided to 'do or die'. The government, on their part, was bent upon crushing the movement by hook or by crook. It was in such a bleak state of affairs that the following correspondence between Gandhiji and Lord Linlithgow (1887–1952), the then Viceroy of India (1936–1943), took place.

1

The Aga Khan's Palace,
Yeravda,
14 August, 1942

Dear Lord Linlithgow,

The Government of India were wrong in precipitating the crisis. The Government resolution justifying the step is full of distortions and misrepresentations. That you have the approval of your Indian 'colleagues' can have no significance, except this that in India you can always command such services. That co-operation is an additional justification for the demand of withdrawal irrespective of what people and parties may say.

The Government of India should have waited at least till the time I inaugurated mass action. I have publicly stated that I fully contemplated sending you a letter before taking concrete action. It was to be an appeal to you for an impartial examination of the Congress case. As you know the Congress has readily filled in every omission that has been discovered in the conception of its demand. So would I have dealt with every deficiency if you had given me the opportunity. The precipitate action of the Government leads one to think that they were afraid that the extreme caution and gradualness with which the Congress was moving towards direct action, might make world opinion ever round to the Congress as it had already begun doing, and expose the hollowness of the grounds for the Government's rejection of the Congress demand. They should surely have waited for an authentic report of my speeches on Friday and on Saturday night after the passing of the resolution by the All-India Congress Committee. You would have found in them that I would not hastily begin action. You would have taken advantage of the interval foreshadowed in them and explored every possibility of satisfying the Congress demand.

The resolution says, 'The Government of India have waited patiently in the hope that wiser counsels might prevail. They have been disappointed in that hope.' I suppose 'wiser counsels' here means abandonment of its demand by the Congress. Why should the abandonment of a demand legitimate at all times be hoped for by a Government pledged to guarantee independence to India? Is it a challenge that could only be met by immediate repression instead of patient reasoning with the demanding party? I venture to suggest that it is a long draft upon the credulity of mankind to say that the acceptance of the demand 'would plunge India into confusion'. Any way the summary rejection of the demand has plunged the nation and the Government into confusion. The Congress was making every effort to identify India with the Allied cause.

The Government resolution says: 'The Governor- General in Council has been aware, too, for some time past, of dangerous preparations by the Congress party for unlawful and in some cases violent activities, directed among other things to the interruption of communications and public utility services, the organization of strikes, tampering with the loyalty of Government servants and interference with defence measures including recruitment.' This is a gross distortion of the reality. Violence was never contemplated at any stage. A definition of what could be included in non-violent action has been interpreted in a sinister and subtle manner as if the Congress was preparing for violent action. Everything was openly discussed among Congress circles, for nothing was to be done secretly. And why is it tampering with your loyalty if I ask you to give up a job that is harming the British people? Instead of publishing behind the backs of principal Congressmen the misleading paragraph, the Government of India, immediately they came to know of the 'preparations', should have brought to book the parties concerned with the preparations. That would have been the appropriate course. By their unsupported allegations in the resolution, they have laid themselves open to the charge of unfair dealing.

The whole Congress movement was intended to evoke in the people the measure of sacrifice sufficient to compel attention. It was intended to demonstrate what measure of popular support it had. Was it wise at this time of the day to seek to suppress a popular Government avowedly non-violent?

The Government resolution further says: 'The Congress is not India's mouthpiece. Yet in the interest of securing their own dominance and in pursuit of their own totalitarian policy its leaders have consistently impeded the efforts made to bring India to full nationhood.' It is a gross libel thus to accuse the oldest national organization of India. This language lies ill in the mouth of a Government which has, as can be proved from public records, consistently thwarted every national effort for attaining freedom, and sought to suppress the Congress by hook or by crook.

The Government of India have not condescended to consider the Congress offer that if simultaneously with the declaration of Independence of India, they could not trust the Congress to form a stable provisional Government, they should ask the Muslim League to do so and that any National Government formed by the League would be loyally accepted by the Congress. Such an offer is hardly consistent with the charge of totalitarianism against the Congress.

Let me examine the Government offer. 'It is that, as soon as hostilities cease, India shall devise for herself, with full freedom of decision and on a basis embracing all and not only a single party, the form of Government which she regards as most suited to her conditions.' Has this offer any reality about it? All parties have not agreed now. Will it be any more possible after the war? And if the parties have to act before Independence is in their hands? Parties grow up like mushrooms, for without proving their representative character, the Government will welcome them as they have done in the past, if the parties oppose the Congress and its activities, though they may do lip-homage to Independence, frustration is inherent in the Government offer. Hence the logical cry of withdrawal first. Only after the end of British power and fundamental change in the political status of India from bondage to freedom, will the formation of a truly representative government, whether provisional or permanent, be possible. The living burial of the authors of the demand has not resolved the deadlock. It has aggravated.

Then the resolution proceeds: 'The suggestion put forward by the Congress party that the millions of India, uncertain as to the future are ready, despite the sad lessons of so many martyr countries, to throw themselves into the arms of the invaders is one that the Government of India cannot accept as a true representation of the feeling of the people of this great country.' I do not know about the millions. But I can give my own evidence in support of the Congress statement. It is open to the Government not to believe the Congress evidence. No imperial power likes to be told that it is in peril. It is because the Congress is anxious for Great Britain to avoid the fate that has overtaken other imperial powers that it asks her to shed imperialism voluntarily by declaring India independent. The Congress has not approached the movement with any but the friendliest motive. The Congress seeks to kill imperialism as much for the sake of the British people and humanity as for India. Notwithstanding assertions to the contrary, I maintain that the Congress has no interests of its own apart from that of the whole of India and the world.

The following passage from the peroration in the resolution is interesting. 'But on them (the Government) there lies the task of defending India, of maintaining India's capacity to wage war, of safeguarding India's interests, of holding the balance between the different sections of her people without fear or favour.'

All I can say is that it is a mockery of truth after the experience in Malaya, Singapore and Burma. It is sad to find the Government of India claiming to hold the 'balance' between the parties for whose creation and existence it is itself demonstrably responsible.

One thing more. The declared cause is common between the Government of India and us. To put it in the most concrete terms, it is the protection of the freedom of China and Russia. The Government of India think that freedom of India is not necessary for winning the cause. I think exactly the opposite. I have taken Jawaharlal Nehru as my measuring rod. His personal contacts make him feel much more the misery of the impending ruin of China and Russia than I can, and may I say than even you can. In that misery he tried to forget his old quarrel with Imperialism. He dreads much more than I do the success of Fascism and Nazism. I argued with him for days together. He fought against my position with a passion which I have no words to describe. But the logic of facts overwhelmed him.

He yielded when he saw clearly that without the freedom of India that of the other two was in great jeopardy. Surely you are wrong in having imprisoned such a powerful friend and ally.

If not withstanding the common cause, the Government's answer to the Congress demand is hasty repression, they will not wonder if I draw the inference that it was not so much the Allied cause that weighed with the British Government, as the unexpressed determination to cling to the possession of India as an indispensable part of imperial policy. The determination led to the rejection of the Congress demand and precipitated repression.

The present mutual slaughter on a scale never before known to history is suffocating enough. But the slaughter of truth accompanying the butchery and enforced by the falsity of which the resolution is reeking adds strength to the Congress position.

It causes me deep pain to have to send you this long letter. But however much I dislike your action, I remain the same friend you have known me. I would still plead for reconsideration of the Government of India's whole policy. Do not disregard the pleading of one who claims to be a sincere friend of the British people. Heaven guide you!

I am,

Yours sincerely,
M.K. Gandhi

2

Dear Lord Linlithgow,

This is a very personal letter. Contrary to the biblical injunction I have allowed many suns to set on a quarrel I have harboured against you. But I must not allow the old year to expire without disburdening myself of what is rankling in my breast against you. I have thought we were friends and should still love to think so. However what has happened since August 9 last makes me wonder whether you still regard me as a friend. I have perhaps not come in such close touch with any occupant of your gadi as with you.

Your arrest of me, the communique you issued thereafter, your reply to Rajaji and the reasons given therefore, Mr Amery's attack on me, and much else I can catalogue go to show that at some stage or other you must have suspected my bona fides. Mention of other Congressmen in the same connection is by the way. I seem to be the fons et origo of all the evil imputed to the Congress. If I have not ceased to be your friend why did you not, before taking drastic action, send for me, tell me of your suspicions and make yourself sure of your facts? I am quite capable of seeing myself as others see me. But in this case I have failed hopelessly. I find that all the statements made about me in Government quarters in this connection contain palpable departures from truth. I have so much fallen from grace that I could not establish contact with a dying friend. I mean Prof. Bhansali who is fasting in regard to the

Chimur affair!!!

And I am expected to condemn the so-called violence of some people reputed to be Congressmen, although I have no data for such condemnation save the heavily censored reports of newspapers. I must own that I thoroughly distrust those reports. I could write much more, but I must not lengthen my tale of woe. I am sure, what I have said is enough to enable you to fill in details.

You know I returned to India from South Africa at the end of 1914 with a mission which came to me in 1906, namely, to spread truth and non-violence among mankind in the place of violence and falsehood in all walks of life. The law of Satyagraha knows no defeat. Prison is one of the many ways of spreading the message. But it has its limits. You have placed me in a palace where every reasonable creature comfort is ensured. I have freely partaken of the latter purely as a matter of duty, never as a pleasure, in the hope that someday those who have the power will realize that they have wronged innocent men. I had given myself six months. The period is drawing to a close. So is my patience. The law of Satyagraha as I know it prescribes a remedy in such moments of trial. In a sentence, it is, 'Crucify the flesh by fasting.' That same law forbids its use except as a last resort. I do not want to use it if I can avoid it.

This is the way to avoid it, convince me of my error or errors, and I shall make ample amends. You can send for me or send someone who knows your mind and can carry conviction. There are many other ways if you have the will. May I expect an early reply? May the New Year bring peace to us all!

I am,

Yours sincerely,
M.K. Gandhi

3

Dear Mr Gandhi,

Thank you for your personal letter of December 31st, which I have just received. I fully accept its personal character, and I welcome its frankness. And my reply will be, as you would wish it to be, as frank and as entirety personal as your letter itself.

I was glad to have your letter, for, to be as open with you as our previous relations justify, I have been profoundly depressed during recent months first by the policy that was adopted by the Congress in August; secondly, because while that policy gave rise, as it was obvious it must, throughout the country to violence and crime (I say nothing of the risks to India from outside aggression) no word of condemnation for that violence and crime should have come from you, or from the Working Committee. When you were first at Poona I knew that you were not receiving newspapers, and I accepted that as explaining your silence. When arrangements were made that you and the Working Committee should have such newspapers as you desired I felt certain that the details those newspapers contained of what was happening would shock and distress you as much as it has us all, and that you would be anxious to make your condemnation of it categorical and widely known. But that was not the case; and it has been a real disappointment to me, all the more when I think of these murders, the burning alive of police officials, the wrecking of trains, the destruction of property, the misleading of these young students, which has done so much harm to India's good name, and to the Congress Party. You may take it from me that the newspaper accounts you mention are well founded—I only wish they were not, for the story is a bad one. I well know the immense weight of your great authority in the Congress movement and with the Party and those who follow its lead, and I wish I could feel, again speaking very frankly, that a heavy responsibility did not rest on you. (And unhappily, while the initial responsibility rests with the leaders, others have to bear the consequences, whether as law breakers, with the results that that involves, or as the victims.)

But if I am right in reading your letter to mean that in the light of what has happened you wish now to retrace your steps and dissociate yourself from the policy of last summer, you have only to let me know and I will at once consider the matter further. And if I have failed to understand your object, you must not hesitate to let me know without delay in what respect I have done so, and tell me what positive suggestion you wish to put to me. You know me well enough after these many years to believe that I shall be only too concerned to read with the same close attention as ever any message which I receive from you, to give it the fullest weight and approach it with the deepest anxiety to understand your feelings and your motives.

Yours sincerely,
Linlithgow

4

To Lord Linlithgow
Detention Camp,
19 January, 1943

Dear Lord Linlithgow,

I received your kind letter of the 13th instant yesterday at
2.30 p.m. I had almost despaired of ever hearing from you.
Please excuse my impatience.

Your letter gladdens me to find that I have not lost caste
with you.

My letter of 31st December was a growl against you. Yours
is a counter-growl. It means that you maintain that you were
right in arresting me and you were sorry for the omissions of
which, in your opinion, I was guilty.

The inference you draw from my letter is, I am afraid,
not correct. I have re-read my letter in the light of your
interpretation, but have failed to find your meaning in it. I
wanted to fast and should still want to if nothing comes out
of our correspondence and I have to be a helpless witness to
what is going on in the country including the privations of
the millions owing to the universal scarcity stalking the land.

If I do not accept your interpretation of my letter, you
want me to make a positive suggestion. This, I might, be able
to do, only if you put me among the members of the Working
Committee of the Congress.

If I could be convinced of my error or worse, of which you
are evidently, I should need to consult nobody, so far as my
own action is concerned, to make a full and open confession
and make ample amends. But I have not any conviction

of error. I wonder if you saw my letter to the Secretary to the Government of India (H.D.) of September 23, 1942. I adhere to what I have said in it and in my letter to you of August 14, 1942.

Of course I deplore the happenings that have taken place since 9th August last. But have I not laid the whole blame for them at the door of the Government of India? Moreover, I could not express any opinion on events which I cannot influence or control and of which I have but a one-sided account. You are bound prima facie to accept the accuracy of reports that may be placed before you by your departmental heads. But you will not expect me to do so. Such reports have, before now, often proved fallible. It was that reason that in my letter of 31st December I pleaded with you to convince me of the correctness of the information on which your conviction was based. You will perhaps appreciate my fundamental difficulty in making the statement you have expected me to make.

This however, I can say from the house-top, that I am as confirmed a believer in non-violence as I have ever been. You may not know that any violence on the part of Congress workers, I have condemned openly and unequivocally. I have even done public penance more than once. I must not weary you with examples. The point I wish to make is that on every such occasion I was a free man.

This time, the retracing, as I have submitted, lies with the Government. You will forgive me for expressing an opinion challenging yours. I am certain that nothing but good would have resulted if you had stayed your hand and granted me the interview which I had announced, on the night of August 8, I was to seek. But that was not to be.

Here, may I remind you that the Government of India

have before now owned their mistakes, as for instance, in the Punjab when the late General Dyer was condemned, in the United Provinces when a corner of a mosque in Cawnpore was restored and in Bengal when the Partition was annulled. All these things were done in spite of great and previous mob violence.

To sum up:

If you want me to act singly, convince me that I was wrong and I will make ample amends.

If you want me to make any proposal on behalf of the Congress you should put me among the Congress Working Committee members.

I do plead with you to make up your mind to end the impasse. If I am obscure or have not answered your letter fully, please point out the omissions and I shall make an attempt to give you satisfaction. I have no mental reservation. I find that my letters to you are sent through the Government of Bombay. This procedure must involve some loss of time. As time is of the essence in this matter, perhaps you will issue instructions that my letters to you may be sent directly by the Superintendent of this camp.

I am,

Your sincere friend,
M.K. Gandhi

5

The Viceroy's House,
New Delhi,
25 January 1943

Dear Mr Gandhi,

Many thanks for your personal letter of the 19th January, which I have just received, and which I need not say I have read with close care and attention. But I am still, I fear, rather in the dark. I made clear to you in my last letter that, however reluctantly, the course of events, and my familiarity with what has been taking place, has left me no choice but to regard the Congress movement, and you as its authorized and fully empowered spokesman at the time of the decision of last August, as responsible for the sad campaign of violence and crime, and revolutionary activity which has done so much harm, and so much injury to India's credit, since last August. I note what you say about non-violence. I am very glad to read your unequivocal condemnation of violence, and I am well aware of the importance which you have given to that article of your creed in the past. But the events of these last months, and even the events that are happening today, show that it has not met with the full support of certain at any rate of your followers, and the mere fact that they may have fallen short of an ideal which you have advocated is no answer to the relations of those who have lost their lives, and to those themselves who have lost their property or suffered severe injury as a result of violent activities on the part of Congress and its supporters. And I cannot I fear accept as an answer your suggestion that 'the whole blame' has been laid by you yourself at the door of the Government of India. We are dealing with facts in this matter, and they have to be faced. And while, as I made clear in my last letter, I am very anxious to have from you anything that you may have to say or any specific proposition that you may have to make, the position remains that it is not the Government of India, but Congress and yourself that are on their justification in this matter.

If therefore you are anxious to inform me that you repudiate or dissociate yourself from the resolution of the 9th August and the policy which that resolution represents, and if you can give me appropriate assurances as regards the future, I shall, I need not say, be very ready to consider the matter further. It is of course very necessary to be clear on that point and you will not, I know, take it amiss that should make that clear in the plainest possible words.

I will ask the Governor of Bombay to arrange that any communication from you should be sent through him, which will I trust reduce delay in its transmission.

Yours sincerely,
Linlithgow

6

Dear Lord Linlithgow,

I must thank you warmly for your prompt reply to my letter of the 19th instant.

I wish I could agree with you that your letter is clear. I am sure you do not wish to imply by clearness simply that you hold a particular opinion strongly. I have pleaded and would continue to plead till the last breath that you should at least make an attempt to convince me of the validity of the opinion you hold, that the August resolution of the Congress is responsible for the popular violence that broke out on the 9th August last and after, even though it broke out after the wholesale arrest of principal Congress workers. Was not the drastic and unwarranted action of the Government responsible for the reported violence? You have not even said what part of the August resolution is bad or offensive in your opinion. That resolution is in no way a retraction by the Congress of its policy of non-violence. It is definitely against Fascism in every shape or form. It tenders co-operation in war effort under circumstances which alone can make effective and nationwide co-operation possible.

The Government have evidently ignored or overlooked the very material fact that the Congress, by its August resolution, asked nothing for itself. All its demands were for the whole people. As you should be aware, the Congress was willing and prepared for the Government inviting Quaid-i-Azam Jinnah to form a national government subject to such agreed adjustments as may be necessary for the duration of the war, such government being responsible to a duly elected assembly.

Being isolated from the Working Committee, except Shrimati Sarojini Devi, I do not know its present mind. But the Committee is not likely to have changed its mind.

Is all this open to reproach?

Objection may be raised to that clause of the resolution which contemplated civil disobedience. But that by itself cannot constitute an objection since the principle of civil disobedience is impliedly conceded in what is known as the 'Gandhi-Irwin Pact'. Even that civil disobedience was not to be started before knowing the result of the meeting for which I was to seek from you an appointment.

Then, take the unproved and in my opinion unprovable charges hurled against the Congress and me by so responsible a Minister as the Secretary of State for India.

Surely I can say with safety that it is for the Government to justify their action by solid evidence, not by mere ipse dixit.

But you throw in my face the facts of murders by persons reputed to be Congressmen. I see the fact of the murders as clearly, I hope, as you do. My answer is that the Government goaded the people to the point of madness. They started leonine violence in the shape of the arrests already referred to. That violence is not any the less so, because it is organized on a scale so gigantic that it displaces the Mosaic Law of tooth for tooth by that of ten thousand for one—not to mention the corollary of the Mosaic Law, i.e., of non-resistance as enunciated by Jesus Christ. I cannot interpret in any other manner the repressive measures of the all-powerful Government of India.

Add to this tale of woe the privations of the poor millions due to India-wide scarcity which I cannot help thinking might have been largely mitigated, if not altogether prevented, had there been a bona fide National Government responsible to a popularly elected Assembly.

If then I cannot get soothing balm for my pain, I must resort to the law prescribed for Satyagrahis, namely, a fast according to capacity. I must commence after the early morning breakfast of the 9th February, a fast for 21 days ending on the morning of the 2nd March. Usually during my fasts, I take water with the addition of salts. But nowadays, my system refuses water. This time therefore I propose to add juices of citrus fruits to make water drinkable. For, my wish is not to fast unto death, but to survive the ordeal, if God so wills. The fast can be ended sooner by the Government giving the needed relief.

I am not marking this letter personal, as I did the two previous ones. They were in no way confidential. They were a mere personal appeal.

I am,

Your sincere friend,
M.K. Gandhi

7

Dear Mr Gandhi,

Many thanks for your letter of 29th January which I have just received. I have read it, as always, with great care and with every anxiety to follow your mind and to do full justice to your argument. But I fear that my view of the responsibility of Congress and of yourself personally for the lamentable disorders of last autumn remains unchanged.

In my last letter I said that my knowledge of the facts left me no choice but to regard the Congress movement, and you as its authorized and fully empowered leader at the time of the decision of last August, as responsible for the campaign of violence and crime that subsequently broke out. In reply you have reiterated your request that I should attempt to convince you that my opinion is correct. I would readily have responded earlier to that request were it not that your letters gave no indication, such as I should have been entitled to expect, that you sought the information with an open mind. In each of them you have expressed profound distrust of the published reports of the recent happenings, although in your last letter, on the basis of the same information, you have not hesitated to lay the whole blame for them on the Government of India. In the same letter you have stated that I cannot expect you to accept the accuracy of the official reports on which I rely. It is not therefore clear to me how you expect or even desire me to convince you of anything. But in fact, the Government of

148

India have never made any secret of their reasons for holding the Congress and its leaders responsible for the deplorable acts of violence, sabotage and terrorism that have occurred since the Congress resolution of the 8th August declared a 'mass struggle' in support of its demands, appointed you as its leader and authorized all Congressmen to act for themselves in the event of interference with the leadership of the movement. A body which passes a resolution in such terms is hardly entitled to disclaim responsibility for any events that follow it. There is evidence that you and your friends expected this policy to lead to violence; and that you were prepared to condone it; and that the violence that ensued formed part of concerted plan, conceived long before the arrest of Congress leaders. The general nature of the case against the Congress has been publicly stated by the Home Member in his speech in the Central Legislative Assembly on the 15th September last, and if you need further information I would refer you to it. I enclose a complete copy in case the press versions that you must have seen were not sufficient. I need only add that all the mass of evidence that has come to light has confirmed the conclusions then reached. I have ample information that the campaign of sabotage has been conducted under secret instructions, circulated in the name of the A.I.C.C; that well-known Congressmen have organized and freely taken part in acts of violence and murder; and that even now an underground Congress organization exists in which, among others, the wife of a member of the Congress Working Committee plays a prominent part, and which is actively engaged in planning the bomb outrages and other acts of terrorism that have disgusted the whole country. If we do not act on all this information or make it publicly known it is because the time is not yet ripe; but you may rest assured that the charges against the Congress will have to be met sooner or later and it will then be for you and your colleagues to clear yourselves before the world if you can. And if in the meanwhile you yourself, by any action such as you now appear to be contemplating, attempt to find an easy way out, the judgement will go against you by default.

I have read with surprise your statement that the principle of civil disobedience is implicitly conceded in the Delhi settlement of the 5th March 1931 which you refer to as the 'Gandhi-Irwin Pact'. I have again looked at the document. Its basis was that civil disobedience would be 'effectively discontinued' and that certain 'reciprocal action' would be taken by Government. It was inherent in such a document that it should take notice of the existence of civil disobedience. But I can find nothing in it to suggest that civil disobedience was recognized as being in any circumstances legitimate. And I cannot make it too plain that it is not so regarded by my Government.

To accept the point of view which you put forward would be to concede that the authorized Government of the country, on which lies the responsibility for maintaining peace and good order, should allow subversive and revolutionary movements described by you yourself as open rebellion, to take place unchallenged; that they should allow preparations for violence, for the interruptions of communications, for attacks on innocent persons, for the murder of police officers and others to proceed unchecked. My Government and I are open indeed to the charge that we should have taken drastic action at an earlier stage against you and against the Congress leaders. But my anxiety and that of my Government has throughout been to give you, and to give the Congress organization, every possible opportunity to withdraw from the position which you have decided to take up. Your statements of last June and July, the original resolution of the Working Committee of the 14th July, and your declaration on the same day that there was no room left for negotiation, and that after all it was an open rebellion are all of them grave and significant, even without your final exhortation to 'do or die'. But with a patience that was perhaps misplaced, it was decided to wait until the resolution of the All-India Congress Committee made it clear that there could be no further toleration of the Congress attitude if Government was to discharge its responsibility to the people of India.

Let me in conclusion say how greatly I regret, having regard to your health and age, the decision that you tell me that you now have in your mind to take. I hope and pray that wiser counsels may yet prevail with you. But the decision whether or not to undertake a fast with its attendant risks is clearly one that must be taken by you alone and the responsibility for which and for its consequences must rest on you alone. I trust sincerely that in the light of what I have said you may think better of your resolution and I would welcome a decision on your part to think better of it, not only because of my own natural reluctance to see you willfully risk your life, but because I regard the use of a fast for political purposes as a form of political blackmail (himsa) for which there can be no moral justification, and understood from your own previous writings that this was also your view.

Yours sincerely,
Linlithgow

8

Dear Lord Linlithgow,

I have to thank you for your long reply dated 5th instant to my letter of 29th January last. I would take your last point first, namely, the contemplated fast which begins on 9th instant. Your letter, from a Satyagrahi's standpoint, is an invitation to fast. No doubt the responsibility for the step and its consequences will be solely mine. You have allowed an expression to slip from your pen for which I was unprepared. In the concluding sentence of the second paragraph you described the step as an attempt 'to find an easy way out'. That you, as a friend, can impute such a base and cowardly motive to me passes comprehension. You have also described it as 'a form of political blackmail', and you quote my previous writings on the subject against me. I abide by my writings. I hold that there is nothing inconsistent in them with the contemplated step. I wonder whether you have yourself read those writings.

I do claim that I approached you with an open mind when I asked you to convince me of my error. A 'profound distrust' of the published reports is in no way inconsistent with my having an open mind.

You say that there is evidence that I (I leave my friends out for the moment) 'expected this policy to lead to violence', that I was 'prepared to condone it', and that 'the violence that ensued formed part of a concerted plan conceived long before the arrest of Congress leaders'. I have seen no evidence in support of such a serious charge. You admit that part of the evidence has yet to be published. The speech of the Home Member, of which you have favoured me with a copy, may be taken as the opening speech of the prosecution counsel and nothing more. It contains unsupported imputations against Congressmen. Of course he has described the violent outburst in graphic language. But he has not said why it took place when it did. I have suggested why it did. You have condemned men and women before trying them and hearing their defence. Surely, there was nothing wrong in my asking you to show me the evidence on which you hold them guilty. What you say in your letter carries no conviction. Proof should correspond to the canons of English Jurisprudence.

If the wife of a member of the Working Committee is actively engaged in 'planning the bomb outrages and other acts of terrorism' she should be tried before a court of law and punished if found guilty. The lady you refer to could only have done the things attributed to her after the wholesale arrests of 9th August last, which I have dared to describe as leonine violence.

You say that the time is not yet ripe to publish the charge against the Congress. Have you ever thought of the possibility of their being found baseless when they are put before an impartial tribunal, or that some of the condemned persons might have died in the meanwhile, or that some of the evidence that the living can produce might become unavailable?

I reiterate the statement that the principle of civil disobedience is implicitly conceded in the settlement of 5th March 1931, arrived at between the then Viceroy on behalf of the Government of India and myself on behalf of the Congress. I hope you know that the principal Congressmen were discharged before that settlement was even thought of. Certain reparations were made to Congressmen under that settlement. Civil disobedience was discontinued only on conditions being fulfilled by the Government. That by itself was, in my opinion, an acknowledgement of its legitimacy, of course under given circumstances. It therefore seems somewhat strange to find you maintain that civil disobedience 'cannot be recognized as being in any circumstances legitimate by your Government'. You ignore the practice of the British Government which has recognized its legitimacy under the name of 'passive resistance'.

Lastly you read into my letters a meaning which is wholly inconsistent with my declaration, in one of them, of adherence to unadulterated non-violence. For, you say in your letter under reply, that 'acceptance of my point of view would be to concede that the authorized Government of the country on which lies the responsibility for maintaining peace and good order, should allow movements to take place, that would admit preparations for violence, interruptions of communications, for attacks on innocent persons, for murders of police officers and others, to proceed unchecked'. I must be a strange friend of yours whom you believe to be capable of asking for recognition of such things as lawful.

I have not attempted an exhaustive reply to the views and statements attributed to me. This is not the place nor the time for such reply. I have only picked out those things which in my opinion demanded an immediate answer. You have left me no loophole for escaping the ordeal I have set before for myself. I begin it on the 9th instant with the clearest possible conscience. Despite your description of it as 'a form of political blackmail', it is on my part meant to be an appeal to the Highest Tribunal for justice which I have failed to secure from you. If I do not survive the ordeal I shall go to the Judgement Seat with the fullest faith in my innocence. Posterity will judge between you as representative of an all-powerful Government and me as a humble man who has tried to serve his country and humanity through it.

My last letter was written against time, and therefore a material paragraph went in as postscript. I now send herewith a fair copy typed by Pyarelal who has taken Mahadev Desai's place. You will find the postscript paragraph restored to the place where it should have been.

I am,

Your sincere friend,
M.K. Gandhi

Lord Mountbatten

Lord Louis Mountbatten (1900–1979), the last Viceroy of India (1947) and the first Governor-General of Independent India (1947–48), was yet another key figure involved in the country's partition and independence. The following letters aptly capture the political turmoil and machinations of the time.

1

In this letter Gandhiji is seen warning Lord Mountbatten, who was the then Viceroy of India, about the legacy of chaos that the Viceroy's actions could create.

On the train to Patna,

8 May, 1947

Dear Friend,

It strikes me that I should summarize what I said and wanted to say and left unfinished for want of time, at our last Sunday's meeting.

I

Whatever may be said to the contrary, it would be a blunder of first magnitude for the British to be party in any way whatsoever to the division of India. If it has to come, let it come after the British withdrawal, as a result of understanding between the parties or [of] an armed conflict which according to Quaid-i-Azam Jinnah is taboo. Protection of minorities can be guaranteed by establishing a court of arbitration in the event of difference of opinion among contending parties.

Meanwhile the Interim Government should be composed either of Congressmen or those whose names the Congress chooses or of Muslim League men or those whom the League chooses. The dual control of today, lacking team work and team spirit, is harmful for the country. The parties exhaust themselves in the effort to retain their seat and to placate you. Want of team spirit demoralizes the Government and imperils the integrity of the services so essential for good and efficient government.

Referendum at the stage in the Frontier (or any province for that matter) is a dangerous thing in itself. You have to deal with the material that faces you. In any case nothing should or can be done over Dr Khan Sahib's head as Premier. Note that this paragraph is relevant only if division is at all to be countenanced.

I feel sure that partition of the Punjab and Bengal is wrong in every case and a needless irritant for the League. This as well as all innovations can come after the British withdrawal not before, except always for mutual agreement. Whilst the British Power is functioning in India, it must be held principally responsible for the preservation of peace in the country. That machine seems to be cracking under the existing strain which is caused by the raising of various hopes that cannot or must not be fulfilled. These have no place during the remaining thirteen months. This period can be most profitably shortened if the minds of all were focused on the sole task of withdrawal. You and you alone can do it to the exclusion of all other activity so far as the British occupation is concerned.

Your task as undisputed master of naval warfare, great as it was, was nothing compared to what you are called to do now. The singlemindedness and clarity that gave you success are much more required in this work.

If you are not to leave a legacy of chaos behind, you have to make your choice and leave the government of the whole of India including the States to one party. The Constituent Assembly has to provide for the governance even of that part of India which is not represented by the Muslim League or some States.

Non-partition of the Punjab and Bengal does not mean that the minorities in these Provinces are to be neglected. In both the Provinces they are large and powerful enough to arrest and demand attention. If the popular Governments cannot placate them the Governors should during the interregnum actively interfere.

The in transmissibility of paramountcy is a vicious doctrine, if it means that they [the States] can become sovereign and a menace for Independent India. All the power wherever exercised by the British in India must automatically descend to its successor. Thus the people of the States become as much part of Independent India as the people of British India. The present Princes are puppets created or tolerated for the upkeep and prestige of the British power. The unchecked powers exercised by them over their people is probably the worst blot on the British Crown. The Princes under the new regime can exercise only such powers as trustees can and as can be given to them by the Constituent Assembly. It follows that they cannot maintain private armies or arms factories. Such ability and statecraft as they possess must be at the disposal of the Republic and must be used for the good of their people and the people as a whole. I have merely stated what should be done with the States. It is not for me to show in this letter how this can be done.

Similarly difficult but not so baffling is the question of the Civil Service. Its members should be taught from now to accommodate themselves to the new regime. They may not be partisans taking sides. The slightest trace of communalism among them should be severely dealt with. The English element in it should know that they owe loyalty to the new regime rather than to the old and therefore to Great Britain. The habit of regarding themselves as rulers and therefore superiors must give place to the spirit of true service of the people.

II

I had a very pleasant two hours and three quarters with Quaid-i-Azam Jinnah on Tuesday last. We talked about the joint statement on non-violence. He was agreeably emphatic over his belief in non-violence. He has reiterated it in the Press statement which was drafted by him.

We did talk about Pakistan-cum-partition. I told him that my opposition to Pakistan persisted as before and suggested that in view of his declaration of faith in non-violence he should try to convert his opponents by reasoning with them and not by show of force. He was, however, quite firm that the question of Pakistan was not open to discussion. Logically, for a believer in non-violence, nothing, not even the existence of God could be outside its scope.

Rajkumari Amrit Kaur saw the first eight paragraphs, the purport of which she was to give to Pandit Nehru with whom I was to send you this letter. But, I could not finish it in New Delhi, I finished it on the train. I hope you and Her Excellency are enjoying your hard-earned rest.

Yours sincerely,
M.K. Gandhi

To
H.E. The Viceroy, Simla

2

Dear Friend,

The Rajkumari has given me the purport of your conversation with her.

Though you have been good enough to tell me that I could see you at any time I wanted to, I must not avail myself of the kindness. I would like, however, to reduce to writing some of the things I hold to be necessary for the proper and swift working of the scheme.

As to the referendum in the Frontier Province I must confess that my idea does not commend itself to Pandit Nehru and his colleagues. As I told you, if my proposal did not commend itself to them, I would not have the heart to go any further with it.

This, however, does not in any way affect my proposal that before proceeding with the referendum, you should invite Quaid-i-Azam Jinnah to proceed to the Frontier Province and to woo the Ministers including Badshah Khan and his Khudai Khidmatgars who have made the Province what it is—better or worse. Before he goes, no doubt, he should be assured of a courteous hearing from them.

Whether he favours the idea or not Quaid-i-Azam should be asked to give a fair picture of the Pakistan scheme before the simple Pathan mind is asked to make its choice of Hindustan or Pakistan. I fancy that the Pathan knows his position in Hindustan. If he does not, the Congress or the Constituent Assembly now at work should be called upon to complete the picture. It will be unfair, I apprehend, to choose between Hindustan or Pakistan without knowing what each is. He should at least know where his entity will be fully protected.

There is as yet no peace in the Frontier Province. Can there be a true referendum when strife has not completely abated? Minds are too heated to think coherently. Neither the Congress nor the League can disown liability for disturbances by their followers. If peace does not reign in the land, the whole superstructure will come to pieces and you will, in spite of division, leave behind legacy of which you will not be proud.

The sooner you have homogeneous ministry the better. In no case can the League nominees work independently of the whole Cabinet. It is a vicious thing that there is no joint responsibility for every act of individual members.

The only way to keep the wonderful time table made by you is to anticipate the future and ask your special staff to work out all the items presented by you without reference to the Cabinet and then when the time comes, the report should be presented to the respective parties for acceptance, amendment or rejection.

The more I see things the more firmly I believe that the States problem presents a variety of difficulties which demand very serious and fearless treatment on your part.

The problem of the civil and military services, though in a way not equally difficult, demands the same firm handling as the States. Gurgaon strife is an instance in point. So far as I know one single officer is responsible for the continuance of the mischief.

Lastly may I suggest that the attempt to please all parties is a fruitless and thankless task. In the course of our conversation I suggested that equal praise bestowed on both the parties was not meant. No praise would have been the right thing. 'Duty will be merit when debt becomes a donation.' It is not too late to mend. Your undoubted skill as a warrior was never more in demand than today. Fancy a sailor without his fleet, save his mother wit!

I have tried to be as succinct as possible. I could not be briefer. If any of the points raised herein demand a personal talk, you have but to appoint the suitable time. Please do not think of calling me for the sake of courtesy.

I received your kind note of 10th instant whilst I had almost finished this note. It does not call for a separate reply.

This was finished at 9.25 p.m. It will be typed tomorrow.

Yours sincerely,
M.K. Gandhi

To
H.E. The Viceroy, Simla

Public Letters

1

To Every Englishman in India

This letter was published in Young India.

Dear Friend,

I wish that every Englishman will see this appeal and give thoughtful attention to it.

Let me introduce myself to you. In my humble opinion, no Indian has co-operated with the British Government more than I have for an unbroken period of twenty-nine years of public life in the face of circumstances that might well have turned any other man into a rebel. I ask you to believe me when I tell you that my co-operation was not based on the fear of the punishments provided by your laws or any other selfish motives. It was free and voluntary co-operation based on the belief that the sum total of the activity of the British Government was for the benefit of India. I put my life in peril four times for the sake of the Empire—at the time of the Boer war when I was in charge of the Ambulance corps whose work was mentioned in General Buller's dispatches, at the time of the Zulu revolt in Natal when I was in charge of a similar corps, at the time of the commencement of the late War when I raised an Ambulance corps and as a result of strenuous training had a severe attack of pleurisy, and lastly, in fulfillment of my promise to Lord Chelmsford at the War Conference in Delhi, I threw myself in such an active recruiting campaign in Kaira District involving long and trying marches, that I had an attack of dysentery, which proved almost fatal.

I did all this in the full belief that acts such as mine must gain for my country an equal status in the Empire. So late as last December I pleaded hard for a trustful co-operation. I fully believed that Mr Lloyd George would redeem his promise to the Mussalmans and that the revelations of the official atrocities in the Punjab would secure full reparation for the Punjabis. But the treachery of Mr Lloyd George and its appreciation by you, and the condonation of the Punjab atrocities have completely shattered my faith in the good intentions of the Government and the nation which is supporting it.

But though my faith in your good intentions is gone, I recognize your bravery, and I know that what you will not yield to justice and reason, you will gladly yield to bravery.

See What This Empire Means to India

Exploitation of India's resources for the benefits of Great Britain, an ever-increasing military expenditure, and a civil service the most expensive in the world, extravagant working of every department in utter disregard of India's poverty, disarmament and consequent emasculation of a whole nation lest an armed nation might imperil the lives of a handful of you in our midst, traffic in intoxicating liquors and drugs for the purpose of sustaining a top-heavy administration, progressively repressive legislation in order to suppress an ever-growing agitation seeking to give expression to a nation's agony, degrading treatment of Indians residing in your dominions and you have shown total disregard of our feelings by glorifying the Punjab administration and flouting the Mussalman sentiment.

I know you would not mind if we could fight and wrest the sceptre from your hands. You know that we are powerless to do that, for you have ensured our incapacity to fight in open and honourable battle. Bravery on the battlefield is thus impossible for us. Bravery of the soul still remains open to us. I know you will respond to that also. I am engaged in evoking that bravery. Non-co-operation means nothing less than training in self-sacrifice. Why should we co-operate with you when we know that by your administration of this great country we are being daily enslaved in an increasing degree? This response of the people to my appeal is not due to my personality. I would like you to dismiss me, and for that matter the Ali Brothers too, from your consideration. My personality will fail to evoke any response to anti-Muslim cry if I were foolish enough to raise it, as the magic name of the Ali Brothers would fail to inspire the Mussalmans with enthusiasm if they were madly to raise an anti-Hindu cry. People flock in their thousands to listen to us because we today represent the voice of a nation groaning under your iron heels. The Ali Brothers were your friends as I was, and still am. My religion forbids me to bear any ill will towards you. I would not raise my hand against you even if I had the power. I expect to conquer you only by my suffering. The Ali Brothers will certainly draw the sword, if they could, in defence of their religion and their country. But they and I have made common cause with the people of India in their attempt to voice their feelings and to find a remedy for their distress.

You are in search of a remedy to suppress this rising ebullition of national feeling. I venture to suggest to you that the only way to suppress it is to remove the causes. You have yet the power. You can repent of the wrongs done to Indians. You can compel Mr Lloyd George to redeem his promises. I assure you he has kept many escape-doors. You can compel the Viceroy to retire in favour of a better one, you can revise your ideas about Sir Michael O'Dwyer and General Dyer. You can compel the Government to summon a conference of the recognized leaders of the people, duly elected by them and representing all shades of opinion so as to revise means for granting Swaraj in accordance with the wishes of the people of India.

But this you cannot do unless you consider every Indian to be in reality your equal and brother. I ask for no patronage, I merely point out to you, as a friend, an honourable solution of a grave problem. The other solution, namely repression, is open to you. I prophesy that it will fail. It has begun already. The Government has already imprisoned two brave men of Panipat for holding and expressing their opinions freely. Another is on his trial in Lahore for having expressed similar opinions. One in the Oudh District is already imprisoned. Another awaits judgement. You should know what is going on in your midst. Our propaganda is being carried on in anticipation of repression. I invite you respectfully to choose the better way and make common cause with the people of India whose salt you are eating. To seek to thwart their aspirations is disloyalty to the country.

I am,

Your faithful friend,
M.K. Gandhi

2

To Every Briton

This was a famous appeal that was issued by Mahatma Gandhi on 3 July, 1940, during World War II. In it, Gandhiji requested every citizen of Britain to work against the war and resume normal relations with other nations.

To Every Briton,

In 1896, I addressed an appeal to every Briton in South Africa on behalf of my countrymen who had gone there as labourers or traders and their assistants. It had its effect. However important it was from my viewpoint, the cause which I pleaded then was insignificant compared with the cause which prompts this appeal. I appeal to every Briton, wherever he may be now, to accept the method of non-violence instead of that of war for the adjustment of the relations between nations and other matters. Your statesmen have declared that this is a war on behalf of democracy. There are many other reasons given in justification. You know them all by heart. I suggest that at the end of the war, whichever way it ends, there will be no democracy left to represent democracy. This war has descended upon mankind as a curse and as a warning. It is a curse, inasmuch as it is brutalizing man on a scale hitherto unknown. All distinctions between combatants and non-combatants have been abolished. No one and nothing is to be spared. Lying has been reduced to an art. Britain was to defend small nationalities. One by one they have vanished, at least for the time being. It also is a warning. It is a warning that, if nobody reads the writing on

170

the wall, man will be reduced to the state of the beast, whom he is shaming by his manners. I read the writing, when the hostilities broke out. But I had not the courage to say the word. God has given me the courage to say it before it is too late.

I appeal for the cessation of hostilities, not because you are too exhausted to fight, but because war is bad in essence. You want to kill Nazism. You will never kill it by its indifferent adoption. Your soldiers are doing the same work of destruction as the Germans. The only difference is that perhaps yours are not as thorough as that of the Germans. And if that be so, yours will soon acquire the same thoroughness as theirs, if not much greater. On no other condition can you win this war. In other words, you will have to be more ruthless than the Nazis. No cause, however just, can warrant the indiscriminate slaughter that is going on minute by minute. I suggest that a cause that demands the inhumanities that are being perpetrated today cannot be called just.

I do not want Britain to be defeated, nor do I want her to be victorious in a trial of brute strength, whether expressed through the muscle or brain. Your muscular bravery is an established fact. Need you demonstrate that your brain is also as unrivalled in destructive power as your muscle? I hope you do not wish to enter into such an undignified competition with the Nazis. I venture to present you with a nobler and braver way, worthy of the bravest soldier. I want you to fight Nazism without arms, or, if I am to retain the military terminology, with non-violent arms. I would like you to lay down the arms you have, as being useless for saving you or humanity. You will invite Herr Hitler and Signor Mussolini to take what they want of the countries you call your possessions. Let them take possession of your beautiful island, with your many beautiful buildings. You will give all these, but neither your souls, nor your minds. If these gentlemen choose to occupy your homes, you will vacate them. If they do not give you free passage out, you will allow yourself, man, woman and child, to be slaughtered, but you will refuse to owe allegiance to them.

This process or this method, which I have called non-violent non-co-operation, is not without considerable success in its use in India. Your representatives in India may deny my claim. If they do, I shall feel sorry for them. They may tell you that our non-co-operation was not wholly non-violent, that it was born of hatred. If they give that testimony, I will not deny it. Had it been wholly non-violent, if all non-co-operators had been filled with goodwill towards you, I make bold to say that you who are India's masters would have become her pupils and, with much greater skill than we have, perfected this matchless weapons and met the German and Italian friends' menace with it. Indeed the history of Europe during the past few months would then have been written differently and Europe would have been spared seas of innocent blood, the rape of so many small nations, and the orgy of hatred.

This is no appeal made by a man who does not know his business. I have been practising with scientific precision non-violence and its possibilities for an unbroken period of over fifty years. I have applied it in every walk of life, domestic and institutional, economic and political. I know of no single case in which it has failed. Where it has seemed sometimes to have failed, I have ascribed it to my imperfections. I claim no perfection for myself. But I do claim to be a passionate seeker after Truth, which is but another name for God. In the course of that search, discovery of non-violence came to me. Its spread is my life mission. I have no interest in living except for the prosecution of that mission.

I claim to have been a life-long and wholly disinterested friend of the British people. At one time I used to be also a lover of your empire. I thought that it was doing good to India. When I saw that in the nature of things it could do no good, I used, and am still using, the non-violent method to fight imperialism. Whatever the ultimate fate of my country, my love for you remains, and will remain, undiminished. My non-violence demands universal love, and you are not a small part of it. It is that love which has prompted my appeal to you.

May God give power to every word of mine. In His name, I began to write this, and in His name I close it. May your statesmen have the wisdom and the courage to respond to my appeal. I am telling His Excellency the Viceroy that my services are at the disposal of His Majesty's Government should they consider them of any practical use in advancing the object of my appeal.

M.K. Gandhi

4

To Every Briton

In this letter addressed to the entire British nation and dated 11 May 1942, Gandhij is seen asking for a peaceful end to British rule in India. He was well aware of the fondness of Britishers to retain old values and cultures, and as such was very careful in drafting this letter.

When I had just begun my public career in South Africa, I wrote 'An Open Letter to Every Briton in South Africa'. It had its effect. I feel that I should repeat the example at this critical juncture in the history of the world. This time my appeal must be to every Briton in the world. He may be nobody in the counsels of his nation. But in the empire of non-violence every true thought counts, every true voice has its full value. Vox populi vox dei is not a copy-book maxim. It is an expression of the solid experience of mankind. But it has one qualification. Its truth is confined to the field of non-violence. Violence can for the moment completely frustrate a people's voice. But since I work on the field of non-violence only, every true thought expressed or unexpressed counts for me.

I ask every Briton to support me in my appeal to the British at this very hour to retire from every Asiatic and African possession and at least from India. That step is essential for the safety of the world and for the destruction of Nazism and Fascism. In this I include Japan's 'ism' also. It is a good copy of the two. Acceptance of my appeal will confound all the military plans of all the Axis Powers and even of the military advisers of Great Britain.

If my appeal goes home, I am sure the cost of British interests in India and Africa would be nothing compared to the present ever-growing cost of the war to Britain. And when one puts morals in the scales, there is nothing but gain to Britain, India and the world.

Though I ask for their withdrawal from Asia and Africa, let me confine myself for the moment to India. British statesmen talk glibly of India's participation in the war. Now India was never even formally consulted on the declaration of war. Why should it be? India does not belong to Indians. It belongs to the British. It has been even called a British possession. The British practically do with it as they like. They make me—an all-war resister—pay a war tax in a variety of ways. Thus I pay two pice as war tax on every letter I post, one pice on every postcard, and two annas on every wire I send. This is the lightest side of the dismal picture. But it shows British ingenuity If I was a student of economics, I could produce startling figures as to what India has been made to pay towards the war apart from what are miscalled voluntary contributions. No contribution made to a conqueror can be truly described as voluntary. What a conqueror the Briton makes! He is well saddled in his seat. I do not exaggerate when I say that a whisper of his wish is promptly answered in India. Britain may, therefore, be said to be at perpetual war with India which she holds by right of conquest and through an army of occupation. How does India profit by this enforced participation in Britain's war? The bravery of Indian soldiers profits India nothing.

Before the Japanese menace overtakes India, India's homesteads are being occupied by British troops—Indian and non-Indian. The dwellers are summarily ejected and expected to shift for themselves. They are paid a paltry vacating expense which carries them nowhere. Their occupation is gone. They have to build their cottages and search for their livelihood. These people do not vacate out of a spirit of patriotism. When this incident was referred to me a few days ago, I wrote in these columns that the dispossessed people should be asked to bear their lot with resignation. But my co-workers protested and invited me to go to the evacuees and console them myself or send someone to perform the impossible task. They were right. These poor people should never have been treated as they were. They should have been lodged suitably at the same time that they were asked to vacate.

People in East Bengal may almost be regarded as amphibious. They live partly on land and partly on the waters of the rivers. They have light canoes which enable them to go from place to place. For fear of the Japanese using the canoes the people have been called upon to surrender them. For a Bengali to part with his canoe, is almost like parting with his life. So those who take away his canoe he regards as his enemy.

Great Britain has to win the war. Need she do so at India's expense? Should she do so?

But I have something more to add to this sad chapter. The falsity that envelops Indian life is suffocating. Almost every Indian you meet is discontented. But he will not own it publicly. The Government employees high and low are no exception. I am not giving hearsay evidence. Many British officials know this. But they have evolved the art of taking work from such elements. This all-pervading distrust and falsity make life worthless unless one resists it with one's whole soul.

You may refuse to believe all I say. Of course I shall be contradicted. I shall survive the contradictions.

I have stated what I believe to be the truth, the whole

truth and nothing but the truth.

My people may or may not approve of this loud thinking. I have consulted nobody. This appeal is being written during my silence day. I am just now concerned with Britain's action. When slavery was abolished in America many slaves protested, some even wept. But protests and tears notwithstanding, slavery was abolished in law. But the abolition was the result of a bloody war between the South and the North; and so though the Negro's lot is considerably better than before, he still remains the outcaste of high society. I am asking for something much higher. I ask for a bloodless end of an unnatural domination and for a new era, even though there may be protests and wailing from some of us.

M.K. Gandhi
Bombay, 11–5-'42

5

To Every Japanese

An open letter addressed to the nation of Japan, wherein Gandhiji severely criticized Japanese aggression against China.

I must confess at the outset that, though I have no ill-will against you, I intensely dislike your attack upon China. From your lofty height you have descended to imperial ambition. You will fail to realize that ambition and may become the authors of the dismemberment of Asia, thus unwittingly preventing world federation and brotherhood without which there can be no hope for humanity.

Ever since I was a lad of eighteen studying in London over fifty years ago, I learnt, through the writings of the late Sir Edwin Arnold, to prize the many excellent qualities of your nation. I was thrilled when in South Africa I learnt of your brilliant victory over Russian arms. After my return to India from South Africa in 1915, I came in close touch with Japanese monks who lived as members of our Ashram from time to time. One of them became a valuable member of the Ashram in Sevagram, and his application to duty, his dignified bearing, his unfailing devotion to daily worship, affability, unruffledness under varying circumstances, and his natural smile which was positive evidence of his inner peace had endeared him to all of us. And now that owing to your declaration of war against Great Britain he has been taken away from us, we miss him as a dear coworker. He has left behind him as a memory his daily prayer and his little drum, to the accompaniment of which we open our morning and evening prayers.

In the background of these pleasant recollections I grieve deeply as I contemplate what appears to me to be your unprovoked attack against China and, if reports are to be believed, your merciless devastation of that great and ancient land.

It was a worthy ambition of yours to take equal rank with the Great Powers of the world. Your aggression against China and your alliance with the Axis Powers was surely an unwarranted excess of that ambition.

I should have thought that you would be proud of the fact that that great and ancient people, whose old classical literature you have adopted as your own, are your neighbours. Your understanding of one another's history, tradition, literature should bind you as friends rather than make you the enemies you are today.

If I was a free man, and if you allowed me to come to your country, frail though I am, I would not mind risking my health, may be my life, to come to your country to plead with you to desist from the wrong you are doing to China and the world and therefore to yourself.

But I enjoy no such freedom. And we are in the unique position of having to resist imperialism that we detest no less than yours and Nazism. Our resistance to it does not mean harm to the British people. We seek to convert them. Ours is an unarmed revolt against British rule. An important party in the country is engaged in a deadly but friendly quarrel with the foreign rulers.

But in this they need no aid from foreign Powers. You have been gravely misinformed, as I know you are, that we have chosen this particular moment to embarrass the Allies when your attack against India is imminent. If we wanted to turn Britain's difficulty into our opportunity we should have done it as soon as the war broke out nearly three years ago.

Our movement demanding the withdrawal of the British Power from India should in no way be misunderstood. In fact, if we are to believe your reported anxiety for the independence of India, a recognition of that independence by Britain should leave you no excuse for any attack on India. Moreover, the reported profession sorts ill with your ruthless aggression against China.

I would ask you to make no mistake about the fact that you will be sadly disillusioned if you believe that you will receive a willing welcome from India. The end and aim of the movement for British withdrawal is to prepare India, by making her free for resisting all militarist and imperialist ambition, whether it is called British Imperialism, German Nazism, or your pattern. If we do not, we shall have been ignoble spectators of the militarization of the world in spite of your belief that in non-violence we have the only solvent of the militarist spirit and ambition. Personally I fear that without declaring the independence of India the Allied Powers will not be able to beat the Axis combination which has raised violence to the dignity of a religion. The Allies cannot beat you and your partners unless they beat you in your ruthless and skilled warfare. If they copy it their declaration that they will save the world for democracy and individual freedom must come to naught. I feel that they can only gain strength to avoid copying your ruthlessness by declaring and recognizing now the freedom of India, and turning sullen India's forced co-operation into freed India's voluntary co-operation.

To Britain and the Allies we have appealed in the name of justice, in proof of their professions, and in their own self-interest. To you I appeal in the name of humanity. It is a marvel to me that you do not see that ruthless warfare is nobody's monopoly. If not the Allies some other Power will certainly improve upon your method and beat you with your own weapon. Even if you win you will leave no legacy to your people of which they would feel proud. They cannot take pride in a recital of cruel deeds however skillfully achieved.

Even if you win it will not prove that you were in the right, it will only prove that your power of destruction was greater. This applies obviously to the Allies too, unless they perform now the just and righteous act of freeing India as an earnest and promise of similarly freeing all other subject peoples in Asia and Africa.

Our appeal to Britain is coupled with the offer of Free India's willingness to let the Allies retain their troops in India. The offer is made in order to prove that we do not in any way mean to harm the Allied cause, and in order to prevent you from being misled into feeling that you have but to step into the country that Britain has vacated. Needless to repeat that if you cherish any such idea and will carry it out, we will not fail in resisting you with all the might that our country can muster. I address this appeal to you in the hope that our movement may even influence you and your partners in the right direction and deflect you and them from the course which is bound to end in your moral ruin and the reduction of human beings to robots.

The hope of your response to my appeal is much fainter than that of response from Britain. I know that the British are not devoid of a sense of justice and they know me. I do not know you enough to be able to judge. All I have read tells me that you listen to no appeal but to the sword. How I wish that you are cruelly misrepresented and that I shall touch the right chord in your heart! Any way I have an undying faith in the responsiveness of human nature. On the strength of that faith I have conceived the impending movement in India, and it is that faith which has prompted this appeal to you.

Sevagram,
18–7–1942
I am,

Your friend and well-wisher,
M.K. Gandhi

6

To American Friends

Britain and America were allies when Gandhiji launched the Quit India movement. There were attempts to characterize Gandhiji as an 'enemy of peace' because he was putting pressure on Britain to leave India when the English nation was at war with the Axis powers. Through this letter addressed openly to the American people, Gandhiji is seen explaining India's position to America.

Dear Friends,

As I am supposed to be the spirit behind the much discussed and equally well abused resolution of the Working Committee of the Indian National Congress on Independence, it has become necessary for me to explain my position. For I am not unknown to you. I have in America perhaps the largest number of friends in the West—not even excepting Great Britain. British friends knowing me personally are more discerning than the American. In America I suffer from the well-known malady called hero worship. Good Dr Holmes, until recently of the Unity Church of New York, without knowing me personally became my advertising agent. Some of the nice things he said about me I never knew myself. So I receive often embarrassing letters from America expecting me to perform miracles. Dr Holmes was followed much later by the late Bishop Fisher who knew me personally in India. He very nearly dragged me to America but fate had ordained otherwise and I could not visit your vast and great country with its wonderful people.

Moreover, you have given me a teacher in Thoreau, who furnished me through his essay on the 'Duty of Civil Disobedience' scientific confirmation of what I was doing in South Africa. Great Britain gave me Ruskin, whose *Unto This Last* transformed me overnight from a lawyer and city-dweller into a rustic living away from Durban on a farm, three miles from the nearest railway station; and Russia gave me in Tolstoy a teacher who furnished a reasoned basis for my non-violence. He blessed my movement in South Africa when it was still in its infancy and of whose wonderful possibilities I had yet to learn. It was he who had prophesied in his letter to me that I was leading a movement which was destined to bring a message of hope to the down-trodden people of the earth. So you will see that I have not approached the present task in any spirit of enmity to Great Britain and the West. After having imbibed and assimilated the message of *Unto This Last*, I could not be guilty of approving of Fascism or Nazism, whose cult is suppression of the individual and his liberty.

I invite you to read my formula of withdrawal or as it has been popularly called 'Quit India' with this background. You may not read into it more than the context warrants.

I claim to be a votary of truth from my childhood. It was the most natural thing to me. My prayerful search gave me the revealing maxim 'Truth is God' instead of the usual one 'God is Truth'. That maxim enables me to see God face to face as it were. I feel Him pervade every fibre of my being. With this Truth as witness between you and me, I assert that I would not have asked my country to invite Great Britain to withdraw her rule over India, irrespective of any demand to the contrary, if I had not seen at once that, for the sake of Great Britain and the Allied cause, it was necessary for Britain boldly to perform the duty of freeing India from bondage. Without this essential act of tardy justice, Britain could not justify her position before the unmurmuring World Conscience, which is their nevertheless. Singapore, Malaya and Burma taught me that the disaster must not be repeated in India. I make bold to say that it cannot be averted unless Britain trusts the people of India to use their liberty in favour of the Allied cause. By that supreme act of justice Britain would have taken away all cause for the seething discontent of India. She will turn the growing ill-will into active goodwill. I submit that it is worth all the battleships and airships that your wonderworking engineers and financial resources can produce.

I know that interested propaganda has filled your ears and eyes with distorted versions of the Congress position. I have been painted as a hypocrite and enemy of Britain under disguise. My demonstrable spirit of accommodation has been described as my inconsistency, proving me to be an utterly unreliable man. I am not going to burden this letter with proof in support of my assertions. If the credit I have enjoyed in America will not stand me in good stead, nothing I may argue in self-defence will carry conviction against the formidable but false propaganda that has poisoned American ears.

You have made common cause with Great Britain. You cannot therefore disown responsibility for anything that her representatives do in India. You will do a grievous wrong to the Allied cause, if you do not sift the truth from the chaff whilst there is yet time. Just think of it. Is there anything wrong in the Congress demanding unconditional recognition of India's independence? It is being said, 'But this is not the time.' We say, 'This is the psychological moment for that recognition.' For them and then only can there be irresistible opposition to Japanese aggression. It is of immense value to the Allied cause if it is also of equal value to India. The Congress has anticipated and provided for every possible difficulty in the way of recognition. I want you to look upon the immediate recognition of India's independence as a war measure of first class magnitude.

I am,

Your friend,
M.K. Gandhi

On the way to Bombay, 3–8–'42

Letters to Family

1

To Maganlal Gandhi

Gandhiji's cousin, Maganlal Gandhi, helped him with his work in South Africa for about a decade, till 1914. Subsequently, he left with about twenty-five students and lived for a while at Rabindranath Tagore's Santiniketan in Bengal. His death in 1928 at the age of forty-five was a severe blow to Gandhiji.

[After 14 March, 1915]

Bhaishri M.,

You are right in what you think about non-violence. Its essentials are daya, akrodha, aman, etc. Satyagraha is based on non-violence. We saw this clearly in Calcutta and came to the conclusion that we should include it among our vows. The thought led to the further conclusion that we must observe all the yamas and that, if we do so by way of vows, we perceive the inner significance of non-violence. In my talks with hundreds of men here I place the various yamas above everything else.

सियाराम प्रेमपीयूषपूरन होत जनमु न भरतको ।
मुनिमनअगम यमनियमसमदम विषमव्रत आचरतको ॥

I remembered this verse in Calcutta on this occasion and pondered deeply over it. I am absolutely clear in my mind that India's deliverance and ours will be achieved through the observance of these vows.

In observing the vow of non-hoarding, the main thing to be borne in mind is not to store up anything which we do not require. For agriculture, we may keep bullocks, if we use them, and the equipment required for them. Where there is a recurring danger of famine, we shall no doubt store food grains. But we shall always ask ourselves whether bullocks and food grains are in fact needed. We are to observe all the yamas in thought as well, so that we shall grow more secure in them from day to day and come to think of fresh things to renounce. Renunciation has no limit to it. The more we renounce, the more shall we grow in the knowledge of the atman. If the mind continues to move towards renunciation of the desire for hoarding and if in practice we give up hoarding as far as it is physically possible to do, we shall have kept the vow of non-hoarding.

The same is true about non-stealing. Non-hoarding refers to stocking of things not needed. Non-stealing refers to the use of such things. If I need only one shirt to cover myself with but use two, I am guilty of stealing one from another. For, a shirt which could have been of use to someone else does not belong to me. If five bananas are enough to keep me going, my eating a sixth one is a form of theft. Suppose we have a stock of fifty limes, thinking that among us all we would need them. I need only two, but take three because there are so many. This is theft.

Such unnecessary consumption is also a violation of the vow of non-violence. If, with the ideal of non-stealing in view, we reduce our consumption of things we would grow more generous. If we do so, actuated by the ideal of non-violence, we would grow more compassionate. In assuring, as it were, every animal or living thing that it need have no fear on our account, we entertain compassion—love—for it. A man who entertains such love will not find any living being inimical to him, not even in thought. That is the most emphatic conclusion of the Shastras and my experience as well.

The principle underlying all these vows is truth. By deceiving oneself, one may refuse to recognize an act of stealing or hoarding as such. Hence, by taking careful thought we can ensure at every step that truth prevails. Whenever we are in doubt whether a particular thing should be stored or not, the simple rule is not to store it. There is no violation of truth in renunciation. When in doubt about the wisdom of speaking, it is the duty of a man who has taken the vow of truth not to speak.

I want all of you to take only such vows as each one feels inclined to, of his own free will. I always feel that vows are necessary. But everyone may take them only when he himself feels the need and take only such as he wants to. Ramchandra may have been a man of great prowess, performed innumerable feats and killed hundreds of thousands of monsters, but no one would think of him today if he had not had such devoted men as Lakshmana and Bharata to follow him. The point is, if Ramchandra had had no more than extraordinary strength as a fighter, his greatness would have been forgotten after a while. There have been many brave warriors who killed monsters as he did. There has been none among them whose fame and greatness are sung in every home. Ramchandra possessed power of some other kind which he could induce into Lakshmana and Bharata and in virtue of which the latter became great men of austerities. Singing in praise of their austerities, Tulsidasji asked, who else, if Bharata had not been born and practised austerities unattainable even by great sages, would have turned an ignorant man like him to Rama? This is as much as to say that Lakshmana and Bharata were the guardians of Rama's fame, that is, of his teaching. Moreover, austerities are not everything.

For, if Lakshmana went without food or sleep for fourteen years, so did Indrajit. But the latter did not know the true significance of austerities which Lakshmana had learnt from Rama; on the contrary, he possessed a nature which inclined him to misuse the power earned through austerities and so came to be known merely as a monster and suffered defeat at the hands of Lakshmana, the man of self-mastery, a lover of God and seeker of deliverance. In the same way, however great the ideal of Gurudev, if there is no one to implement that ideal, it will remain hidden in the profound darkness of the ages. Conversely, if there are any to put it into practice, it will spread its light multiplied many times over. The steps which one has to climb in order to practise an ideal constitute tapas. One should realize, therefore, how very necessary it is to bring tapas—discipline—into the life of children.

Blessings from,
Bapu

2

To Maganlal Gandhi

Navagam,
Thursday [25 July, 1918]

Chi. Maganlal,

You have been frightened by Raojibhai as he was by me. He read too much into my words.

No, my ideals have not changed. Despite my bitter experiences in India, my conviction remains the same as ever, that we have but little to learn from the West. The evils I have seen here have made no change in my fundamental idea nor has this war. The old idea has developed into something purer. I have certainly not come to feel that we shall have to introduce Western civilization. Nor do I suppose that we shall have to take to drinking and meat-eating. To be sure, I have felt, in all seriousness, that Swaminarayana and Vallabhacharya have robbed us of our manliness. They made the people incapable of self-defence. It was all to the good, of course, that people gave up drinking, smoking, etc.; this, however, is not an end in itself, it is only a means. If a smoker happens to be a man of character his company is worth cultivating. If, on the contrary, a man who has never smoked in his life is an adulterer, he can be of little service. The love taught by Swaminarayana and Vallabh is all sentimentalism. It cannot make one a man of true love. Swaminarayana and Vallabh simply did not reflect over the true nature of non-violence. Non-violence consists in holding in check all impulses in the chitta. It comes into play especially in men's relations with one another. There is not even a suggestion of this idea in their writings. Having been born in this degenerate age of ours, they could not remain unaffected by its atmosphere and had, in consequence, quite an undesirable effect on Gujarat. Tukaram and Ramdas had no such effect. The Abhangas of the former and the shlokas of the latter admit ample scope for manly striving. They, too, were Vaishnavas. Do not mix up the Vaishnava tradition with the teaching of Vallabh and Swaminarayana. Vaishnavism is an age-old truth. I have come to see, what I did not so clearly before, that there is non-violence in violence. This is the big change which has come about. I had not fully realized the duty of restraining a drunkard from doing evil, of killing a dog in agony or one infected with rabies. In all these instances, violence is in fact non-violence. Violence is a function of the body. Brahmacharya consists in refraining from sexual indulgence, but we do not bring up our children to be impotent. They will have observed brahmacharya only if, though possessed of the highest virility, they can master the physical urge. In the same way, our offspring must be strong in physique. If they cannot completely renounce the urge to violence, we may permit them to commit violence, to use their strength to fight and thus make them non-violent. Non-violence was taught by a Kshatriya to a Kshatriya.

The difference between the West and the East is what I have explained to be, and it is a great one. The civilization of the West is based on self-indulgence, ours on self-control. If we commit violence, it will be as a last resort and with a view to lokasangraha. The West will indulge in violence in self-will. My taking part in (the movement for) a Parliament and similar activities is not a new development; it is quite an. old thing and is only intended to ensure a check on these bodies.

You will see this if you read my article on Mr Montagu's scheme. I simply cannot bring myself to take interest in the movement, but I can spread my ideals by working in it. When I saw that I could continue in it only by sacrificing my ideals, I decided to retire from the movement.

I think you have your reply in what I have said. I cannot explain much when I am there for a day and so I have set down the thing in writing. This will enable you to think and ask me questions, if fresh doubts occur to you.

I continue to be in Navagam. I wanted to leave from here today, but perhaps I may not be able to do so.

Blessings from,
Bapu

3

To Kasturba Gandhi

Their work for the nation often forced Gandhiji and his wife, Kasturba Gandhi (1869–1944), a political activist in her own right, to stay away from each other. In this letter, Gandhiji can be seen consoling his wife and helping her deal with their separation.

[Nadiad]
29 July, 1918

Beloved Kastur,

I know you are pining to stay with me. I feel, though, that we must go on with our tasks. At present, it is right that you remain where you are. If you but look upon all the children there as your own, quite soon you will cease to feel the absence of the latter. This is the least one can do as one gets older. As you come to love others and serve them, you will have a joy welling up from within. You should make it a point to visit early in the morning all those who may be sick, and nurse them. Special food should be prepared or kept apart for anyone who needs such food. You should visit the Maharashtrian ladies, amuse their children or take them out for a walk. You should make them feel that they are no strangers. Their health should improve.

You should converse with Nirmala on useful subjects, that is, on religious matters and the like. You may ask her to read out the Bhagavat to you. She will even find the thing interesting. If you thus keep yourself busy in the service of others, believe me the mind will always be full of joy. And you must not omit to look after Punjabhai's meals and other requirements.

Mohandas

Miscellaneous Letters

1

Letter to Dadabhai Naoroji

This extract is from the first of many letters that Gandhiji sent to Dadabhai Naoroji, and is taken from R.E. Masani's Dadabhai Naoroji: The Grand Old Man of India.

Durban,
5 July, 1894

The first Parliament of Natal under Responsible Government has been pre-eminently an Indian Parliament. It has for the most part occupied itself with legislation affecting Indians, by no means favourably. The Governor, in opening the Legislative Council and Assembly, remarked that his Ministers would deal with the Franchise which was exercised by Indians in Natal, although they never exercised it in India. The reasons given for the sweeping measure to disfranchise Indians were that they had never exercised the Franchise before, and that they were not fit for it.

The petition of the Indians seemed to prove a sufficient answer to this. Hence they have now turned round and given out the real object of the Bill, which is simply this: 'We do not want the Indians any more here. We want the coolies, but they shall remain slaves here and go back to India as soon as they are free.' I earnestly request your undivided attention to the cause and appeal to you to use your influence that always has been and is being used on behalf of the Indians, no matter where situated. The Indians look up to you as children to the father. Such is really the feeling here.

A word for myself and I have done. I am yet inexperienced

and young and, therefore, quite liable to make mistakes. The responsibility undertaken is quite out of proportion to my ability. I may mention that I am doing this without any remuneration. So you will see that I have not taken the matter up, which is beyond my ability, in order to enrich myself at the expense of the Indians. I am the only available person who can handle the question. You will, therefore, oblige me very greatly if you will kindly direct and guide me and make necessary suggestions which shall be received as from a father of his child.

2

To Narhar Shambhurao Bhave

Narhar Shambhurao Bhave was Acharya Vinoba Bhave's father.
Vinoba Bhave met Gandhiji on 7 June, 1916, which prompted
Gandhiji to write this short missive.

[Ahmedabad]

Your son Vinoba is with me. Your son has acquired at so
tender an age such high-spiritedness and asceticism as took
me years of patient labour to do.

3

To Mr Maffey, Private Secretary to Viceroy

Gandhiji wrote this letter to the secretary of the then Viceroy of India, Lord Chelmsford, after receiving several reports and complaints about the 'reign of terror' perpetrated by indigo planters in Motihari, Bihar, and subsequently visiting the district. In it, he offers to return the Kaisar-i-Hind medal given to him in 1915 by The Lord Hardinge of Penshurst.

Care District Magistrate,
Motihari,
16 April, 1917

Dear Mr Maffey,

I have come to this district to learn for myself whether there is truth in the allegations of the ryots against the planters. I saw the Secretary of the Planters' Association and then the Commissioner of the Division, and sought their co-operation. Both politely rejected my advances and dissuaded me from my pursuit. I could not accept their advice, and have been proceeding with my work. The Magistrate has served upon me an order asking me to leave the District. The grounds for the order are such as I cannot subscribe to. I have therefore been reluctantly obliged to disobey the order and tell the Magistrate that I shall suffer the penalty for the breach.

My motive is national service and that, too, so long as it is consistent with humanitarian dictates. I understand, because my South African work was considered to be humanitarian that I was awarded the Kaisar-i-Hind Gold Medal. So long as my humanitarian motive is questioned, so long must I remain undeserving of holding the medal. I am therefore asking my people to return the medal to you, and I shall feel honored to receive it back if it is returned to me when my motive is no longer questioned.

As to the question itself, so far as I have been able to examine the evidence, given to me, it shows that the planters have successfully used the Civil and Criminal Courts and illegal force to enrich themselves at the expense of the ryots, and that the ryots are living under a reign of terror and that their property, their persons, and their minds are all under the planters' heels. One man graphically said to me: 'We belong to the planters, not to the Sircar. Thana is nowhere, the planters are everywhere. We take what they allow, and we keep what they permit.' I had hoped that a deeper examination would have toned down the impression formed by me. Had I been left free, I would have concluded my studies and placed the results at the disposal of the authorities. I wish that His Excellency would consider the matter serious enough to have an independent inquiry made.

The local administration admits that they are sitting upon a mine so dangerous that they cannot tolerate my presence. And yet they manage to be satisfied with the slow inquiry of a settlement officer. Everything will depend upon swiftness and the proper choice of the members of the Committee of Inquiry. This is the least that the ryots are entitled to. Will you please place this before the Viceroy and ask for his forgiveness for sending such a long letter in the midst of many imperative calls upon his time. The urgency of the matter is the sole excuse for this letter.

I am, etc.,

M.K. Gandhi

4

To Shankarlal on 'Ideas about Satyagraha'

Shankarlal Ghelabhai Banker was a renowned labour leader of the Gandhian school of thought, who had a long association with Gandhiji himself.

[2 September, 1917]

Bhaishri Shankarlal,

You want to know my ideas about Satyagraha. Here they are in brief:

The English phrase 'passive resistance' does not suggest the power I wish to write about; 'Satyagraha' is the right word. Satyagraha is soul-force, as opposed to armed strength. Since it is essentially an ethical weapon, only men inclined to the ethical way of life can use it wisely. Prahlad, Mirabai, and others were Satyagrahis. At the time of the Morocco fighting, the Arabs were under fire from French guns. The Arabs were fighting, as they believed, solely for their religion. Reckless of their lives, they advanced running towards the French guns with cries of 'Ya Allah'. Here, there was no scope at all for fighting back to kill. The French gunners refused to fire on these Arabs and, throwing up their caps, ran to embrace these brave Arabs with shouts of joy. This is an example of Satyagraha and the success it can achieve. The Arabs were not Satyagrahis by deliberate choice. They got ready to face death under pressure of a strong impulse, and had no love in their hearts. A Satyagrahi bears no ill-will, does not lay down his life in anger, but refuses rather to submit to his 'enemy' or oppressor because he has the strength himself to suffer. He should, therefore, have a courageous spirit and a forgiving and compassionate nature. Imam Hassan and Hussain were merely two boys. They felt that an injustice had been done to them. When called upon to surrender, they refused. They knew at the time that this would mean death for them. If, however, they were to submit to injustice, they would disgrace their manhood and betray their religion. In these circumstances, they yielded to the embrace of death. The heads of these fine young men rolled on the battlefield. In my view, Islam did not attain its greatness by the power of the sword but entirely through the self-immolation of its fakirs. It is soldier-like to allow oneself to be cut down by a sword, not to use the sword on another. When he comes to realize that he is guilty of murder, the killer, if he has been in the wrong, will feel sorry forever afterwards. The victim, however, will have gained nothing but victory even if he had acted wrongly in courting death. Satyagraha is the way of non-violence. It is, therefore, justified, indeed it is the right course, at all times and all places. The power of arms is violence and condemned as such in all religions. Even those who advocate the use of arms put various limits on it. There are no limits on Satyagraha, or rather, none except those placed by the Satyagrahi's capacity for tapascharya, for voluntary suffering.

Obviously, it is irrelevant to raise issues about the legality of such Satyagraha. It is for the Satyagrahi to decide. Observers may judge Satyagraha after the event. The world's displeasure will not deter a Satyagrahi. Whether or not Satyagraha should be started is not decided by any mathematical rule. A man who believes that Satyagraha may be started only after weighing the chances of defeat and victory and assuring oneself of the certainty of victory, may be a shrewd enough politician or an intelligent man, but he is no Satyagrahi. A Satyagrahi acts spontaneously.

Satyagraha and arms have both been in use from time immemorial. We find them praised in the extant scriptures. They are the expressions, one of the daivi sampad and the other of the asuri sampad, We believe that in former times in India the daivi sampad was much the stronger of the two. Even today that is the ideal we cherish. Europe provides the most striking example of the predominance of the asuri sampad.

Both these forms of strength are preferable to weakness, to what we know by the rather plain but much after word 'cowardice'. Without either, Swaraj or genuine popular awakening is impossible. Swaraj achieved otherwise than through resort to one or the other will not be true Swaraj. Such Swaraj can have no effect on the people. Popular awakening cannot be brought about without strength, without manliness. Let the leaders say what they like and the Government strives its utmost, unless they and we, all of us, strengthen the forces of Satyagraha, the methods of violence are bound automatically to gain ascendancy. They are like weeds which grow wild in any soil. The crop of Satyagraha requires willingness to exert oneself or a venturesome spirit by way of manure. Just as, moreover, the seedlings are likely to be lost among the weeds if the latter are not plucked out, so also will weeds of violence keep growing unless we keep the land free of them by tapascharya and, with compassion, pluck out those which have already grown. We can, with the help of Satyagraha win over those young men who have been driven to desperation and anger by what they think to be the tyranny of the Government and utilize their courage and their mettlesome spirit, their capacity for suffering, to strengthen the daivi sampad of Satyagraha. It is therefore very much to be desired that Satyagraha is propagated as quickly as it can be. This is in the interest both of the rulers and the ruled. The Satyagrahi desires to harass neither the Government nor anyone else. He takes no step without the fullest deliberation He is never arrogant. Consequently, he will keep away from 'boycott' but be always firm in the vow of Swadeshi as a matter of duty. He fears God alone, so that no other power can intimidate him. He will never, out of fear of punishment, leave a duty undone.

I need hardly say now that it is our duty to resort to Satyagraha to secure the release of the learned Annie Besant and her co-workers. Whether we approve of every or any action of hers is another question. I, for one, certainly do not approve of some of them; all the same, her incarceration by the Government is a great mistake and an act of injustice. I know, of course, that the Government does not think it a mistake. Maybe the people are wrong in desiring her release. The Government has acted according to its lights. What can the people do to express their outraged feelings? Petitions, etc., are good enough when one's suffering is bearable. When it is unbearable, there is no remedy but Satyagraha. Only when people find it unbearable will they, and only those who find it unbearable will, devote their all, body, mind and possessions, to securing the release of Annie Besant. This will be a powerful expression of popular feeling. It is my unshakable faith that before so great a self-sacrifice even the power of an emperor will give way. People may certainly restrain their feelings in view of the forthcoming visit of Mr Montague. That will be an expression of faith in his sense of justice. If she is not released, however, before his arrival, it will be our duty to resort to Satyagraha. We do not want to provoke the Government or put difficulties in its way. By resorting to Satyagraha, we reveal the intensity of our injured feelings and thereby serve the Government.

5

To Vinoba Bhave

[Sabarmati,
After 10 February, 1918]

I do not know in what terms to praise you. Your love and your character fascinate me and so also your self-examination. I am not fit to measure your worth. I accept your own estimate and assume the position of a father to you. You seem almost to have met a long-felt wish of mine. In my view a father is, in fact, a father only when he has a son who surpasses him in virtue. A real son, likewise, is one who improves on what the father has done; if the father is truthful, firm of mind and compassionate, the son will be all this in a greater measure. This is what you have made yourself. I don't see that you owe your achievement to any effort of mine. Hence, I accept the role you offer to me as a gift of love. I shall strive to be worthy of it; and, if ever I become another Hiranyakashipu, oppose me respectfully as Prahlad, who loved God, disobeyed him.

It is true as you say that, though outside the Ashram, you have scrupulously observed its rules. I never doubted that you would return. Besides, I had your written messages, read out by Mama. May God grant you long life, and use you for the uplift of India.

I don't see any need for changes in your diet just yet. Do not give up milk for the present. On the contrary, increase the quantity, if necessary.

About the railways, no Satyagraha is required.

What is wanted is intelligent workers to carry on

propaganda. In the issue in Kheda District, Satyagraha may possibly have to be offered. I am something of a tramp these days. In a day or two, I shall have to leave for Delhi.

More when you arrive. Everyone is looking forward to seeing you.

Blessings from,
Bapu

6

To Kishorelal Mashruwala

A life long associate of Gandhiji, Kishorelal G. Mashruwala (1890–1952) devoted his life to Gandhian thought and became one of its most definitive interpreters. Alongside writing books on Gandhiji, he worked as an editor at Harijan.

[Nadiad]
29 July, 1918

Dear Kishorelal,

This letter is meant for you and Shri Narahari. To the extent that Shri Narayanarao's charge that distinctions are made between Maharashtrians and Gujaratis is justified, it is our duty to try to remove the causes. Here is a field for the exercise of non-violence. The first step to take is for you all to come together and examine how much of truth there is in the charge. The Gujarati ladies should try to mix freely with the Maharashtrian ladies. The most important thing is to see that the children make no such distinction. It is not necessary to give exaggerated importance to what I have said; just reflect over it for a moment and do all that may need to be done.

As for prayers, I place this before you for consideration. We should not take the plea of inability so far that, in the end, we find ourselves incapable of doing anything at all. We should do the teaching as well as we can and overcome our shortcomings by gradual effort. Do you think I would use the plea of inability if I was myself required to teach Sanskrit? I know that my Sanskrit is no Sanskrit. But I would certainly teach it if no other person was available and I would get over my deficiency day by day. It was in this way that Parnell topped them all in his knowledge of the rules of business in the House of Commons. You always think of your weakness and are afraid of doing anything. Would you not be happier if, using all your strength, you disposed of every task that fell to you?

In what manner should the children learn to use their strength? It is a difficult thing to teach them to defend themselves and yet not be overbearing. Till now, we used to teach them not to fight back if anyone beat them. Can we go on doing so now? What will be the effect of such teaching on a child? Will he, in his youth, be a forgiving or a timid man? My powers of thinking fail me. Use yours. This new aspect of non-violence which has revealed itself to me has enmeshed me in no end of problems. I have not found one master-key for all the riddles, but it must be found. Shall we teach our boys to return two blows for one, or tolerate a blow from anyone weaker than themselves but to fight back, should a stronger one attack them, and take the beating that might follow? What should one do if assaulted by a Government official? Should the boy submit to the beating at the moment and then come to us for advice, or should he do what might seem best in the circumstances and take the consequences? These are the problems which face us if we give up the royal road of turning the other cheek. Is the first course the right one because easier to take? Or is it that we shall come upon the right path only by treading through a dangerous one? The foot-tracks which go up the Himalayas lead in all directions, sometimes even away from the destination and yet an experienced guide will take us in the end to the summit. One cannot climb the Himalayas in a straight line. Can it be that, in like fashion, the path

of non-violence, too, is difficult? May God protect us, may
He indeed.

Vandematram from,
Mohandas

7

To Sarojini Naidu

18 November, 1918

Dear Sister,

I appreciated your little note. I observe that you have survived the operation. I hope that it will be entirely successful, so that India may for many a year to come continue to hear your songs. For me I do not know when I shall be able to leave this sickbed of mine. Somehow or other, I cannot put on flesh and gain more strength than I have. I am making a mighty attack. The doctors of course despair in face of the self-imposed restrictions under which I am labouring. I assure you that they have been my greatest consolation during this protracted illness. I have no desire whatsoever to live upon condition of breaking those disciplinary and invigorating restrictions. For me, although they restrict the body somewhat, they free the soul and they give me a consciousness of it which I should not otherwise possess. 'You can't serve God and Mammon' has a clearer and deeper meaning for me after those vows. I do not infer that they are necessary for all, but they are for me. If I broke them I feel that I should be perfectly worthless.

Do let me have an occasional line from you.

Yours,
M.K. Gandhi

8

To the Viceroy

This letter was addressed to Lord Reading, who served as the Viceroy and Governor-General of India from 1921 to 1926, and was published in Young India.

[Bardoli,
1 February, 1922]

To
His Excellency The Viceroy,
Delhi

Sir,

Bardoli is a small tahsil in the Surat District in the Bombay Presidency, having a population of about 87,000 all told.

On the 29th ultimo, it decided under the presidency of Vithalbhai Patel to embark on mass Civil Disobedience, having proved its fitness for it in terms of the resolution of the All-India Congress Committee which met at Delhi during the first week of November last. But, as I am perhaps chiefly responsible for Bardoli's decision, I owe it to Your Excellency and the public to explain the situation under which the decision has been taken.

It was intended under the Resolution of the All-India Congress Committee before referred to, to make Bardoli the first unit for mass Civil Disobedience in order to mark the national revolt against the Government of India for its consistently criminal refusal to appreciate India's just resolve regarding the Khilafat, the Punjab and Swaraj.

Then followed the unfortunate and regrettable rioting

in Bombay on the 17th November last, resulting in the postponement of the step contemplated by Bardoli.

Meanwhile, repression of virulent type has taken place with the concurrence of the Government of India in Bengal, Assam, the United Provinces, the Punjab, the Province of Delhi and, in a way, in Bihar and Orissa and elsewhere. I know that you have objected to the use of the word 'repression' for describing the action of the authorities in those provinces. In my opinion, when action is taken which is in excess of the requirements of a situation, it is undoubtedly repression. The looting of property, assaults on innocent people, the brutal treatment of prisoners in the jails including flogging can in no sense be described as legal, civilized or in any way necessary. This official lawlessness cannot be described by any other term but lawless repression. Intimidation by Non-co-operators or their sympathizers to a certain extent in connection with hartals and picketing may be admitted, but in no case can it be held to justify the wholesale suppression of peaceful volunteering or equally peaceful public meetings under a distorted use of an extraordinary law which was passed in order to deal with activities which were manifestly violent both in intention and action, nor is it possible to designate, as otherwise than repression, action taken against innocent people under what has appeared to many of us an illegal use of the ordinary law, nor again can the administrative interference with the liberty of the Press under a law that is under promise of repeal be regarded as anything but repression.

The immediate task before the country, therefore, is to rescue, from paralysis freedom of speech, freedom of association and freedom of the Press. In the present mood of the Government of India and in the present unprepared state of the country in respect of complete control of the forces of violence, Non-co-operators were unwilling to have anything to do with the Malaviya Conference whose object was to induce Your Excellency to convene a Round Table Conference. But as I was anxious to avoid all avoidable suffering, I had no hesitation in advising the Working Committee of the Congress to accept the recommendations of that Conference. Although in my opinion the terms were quite in keeping with your own requirements as I understood them through your Calcutta speech and otherwise, you have summarily rejected the proposal.

In the circumstances, there is nothing before the country but to adopt some non-violent method for the enforcement of its demands including the elementary rights of free speech, free association and free Press. In my humble opinion, the recent events are a clear departure from the civilized policy laid down by Your Excellency at the time of the generous, manly and unconditional apology of the Ali brothers, viz., that the Government of India should not interfere with the activities of Non-co-operation so long as they remained non-violent in word and deed. Had the Government's policy remained neutral and allowed public opinion to ripen and have its full effect, it would have been possible to advise postponement of the adoption of civil disobedience of an aggressive type till the Congress had acquired fuller control over the forces of violence in the country and enforced greater discipline among the millions of its adherents. But this lawless repression (in a way unparalleled in the history of this unfortunate country) has made the immediate adoption of mass Civil Disobedience an imperative duty. The Working Committee of the Congress has restricted it to only certain areas to be selected by me from time to time, and at present it is confined only to Bardoli. I may, under the said authority, give my consent at once in respect of a group of hundred villages in Guntur in the Madras Presidency, provided they can strictly conform to the conditions of non-violence, unity among different classes, the adoption and manufacture of hand-spun Khadi and untouchability.

But before the people of Bardoli actually commence mass Civil Disobedience, I would respectfully urge you, as head of the Government of India, finally to revise your policy and set free all the non-co-operating prisoners who are convicted or under trial for non-violent activities, and to declare in clear terms a policy of absolute non-interference with all non-violent activities in the country whether they be regarding the redress of the Khilafat or the Punjab wrongs or Swaraj or any other purpose and even though they fall under the repressive sections of the Penal Code or the Criminal Procedure Code or other repressive laws subject always to the conditions of non-violence. I would further urge you to free the Press from all administrative control and to restore all the fines and forfeitures recently imposed. In thus urging I am asking Your Excellency to do what is being done today in every country which is deemed to be under civilized government. If you can see your way to make the necessary declaration within seven days of the date of publication of this manifesto, I shall be prepared to advise postponement of civil disobedience of an aggressive character, till the imprisoned workers have, after their discharge, reviewed the whole situation and considered the position de novo. If the Government makes the requested declaration, I shall regard it as an honest desire on its part to give effect to public opinion and shall have no hesitation in advising the country to be engaged in further moulding public opinion without violent restraint from either side and trust to its working to secure the fulfillment of its unalterable demands. Aggressive civil disobedience in that case will be taken up only when the Government departs from its policy of strictest neutrality or refuses to yield to clearly expressed opinion of the vast majority of the people of India.

I remain,

Your Excellency's faithful
Servant and friend,
M.K. Gandhi

9

To Jamnalal Bajaj

Jamnalal Bajaj (1889–1942) was an industrialist and freedom fighter. He founded the Bajaj Group of companies, one of India's oldest and most famous conglomerates.

Sabarmati Central Prison,
Thursday Night,
16 March, 1922

Chi. Jamnalal,

As I proceed in my search for truth it grows upon me that Truth comprehends everything. It is not in Ahimsa, but Ahimsa is in it. What is perceived by a pure heart and intellect is truth for that moment. Cling to it, and it enables one to reach pure truth. There is no question there of divided duty. But often enough it is difficult to decide what is Ahimsa. For instance, the use of disinfectants is Himsa, and yet we cannot do without it. We have to live a life of Ahimsa in the midst of a world of Himsa, and that is possible only if we cling to truth. That is how I deduce Ahimsa from truth. Out of truth emanate love, tenderness, humility. A votary of truth has to be humble as the dust. His humility increases with his observance of truth. I see this every moment of my life. I have a much vivider sense of Truth and of my own littleness than I had a year ago. The wonderful implication of the great truth 'Brahma Satyam Jaganmithya (Brahma is real, all else unreal) grows on me from day to day. It teaches us patience. This will purge us of harshness and add to our tolerance. It will make us magnify the mole-hills of our errors into mountains and minimize the mountains of others' errors into mole-hills. The body persists because of egoism. The utter extinction of the body of egoism is moksha. He who has achieved this will be the very image of Truth, or one may call it Brahman. Therefore the loving name of God is Dasanudasa (Servant of Servants).

Wife, children, friends, possessions—all should be held subservient to Truth. Each one of these should be sacrificed in the search for truth. Only then can one be a Satyagrahi. I have thrown myself into this movement with a view to making the observance of this principle comparatively easy, and it is with the same object that I do not hesitate to plunge men like you in it. Its outward form is Hind Swaraj. This Swaraj is being delayed because there is yet to be found a Satyagrahi of that type. This, however, need not dismay us. It should spur us on to greater effort.

You have made yourself my fifth son. But I am striving to be worthy. It is not an ordinary responsibility for an adopter. May God help me, and may I be worthy of it in this very life.

Bapuna Ashirvad

10

To Motilal Nehru

Motilal Nehru (1861–1931) was a lawyer and one of the most important early leaders of the Indian National Congress. He was the father of Jawaharlal Nehru and a close associate of Gandhiji.

Bombay,
2 September, 1924

Dear Motilalji,

This is again early morning after prayer. I hope you received my long letter. I expect a wire from you. I was unable to revise it. I cannot now recall the exact wording of the personal part. After all, Mrs Naidu did not read it as the letter was posted before she could read it. But the business part, of which I have a copy, she and many others have read.

This letter like the former is meant to be a plea for Jawaharlal. He is one of the loneliest young men of my acquaintance in India. The idea of your mental desertion of him hurts me. Physical desertion I hold to be impossible. Needless to say Manzar Ali and I often talked of the Nehrus whilst we were together at Yeravda. He said once that if there was one thing for which you lived more than any other, it was for Jawahar. His remark seemed to be so true. I don't want to be the cause direct or indirect of the slightest breach in that wonderful affection.

Yours sincerely,
M.K. Gandhi

11

To Motilal Nehru

The Ashram, Sabarmati,
20 April, 1928

Dear Motilalji,

I have your letter. I am daily making fresh discoveries which go to show that we may expect nothing from the mill-owners at the present stage. They will yield only to pressure and the pressure of the Government is more felt than that of the Congress. But we may not be impatient. We need not put boycott of Indian mill-made cloth in the same category as that of foreign cloth. A negative attitude about mill cloth will be quite enough to keep the mills under wholesome check. A positive boycott will only stir up bad blood without bringing us any nearer boycott of foreign cloth. We shall never, unless a sudden manifestation of mass energy comes into being, succeed in reaching the millions. In spite of all we may do, for the time being the latter will therefore be buying Indian mill cloth and, further, there will be keen competition between Lancashire mills and Japanese on the one hand and Indian mills on the other. We have therefore to concentrate our effort on changing the mentality of the townspeople and those few villagers whom we are controlling and bringing them round to the adoption of Khadi. If we set about doing this, the message of Khadi will percolate the masses. Then both our and foreign mills will feel the brunt. That will be the time for our mills to come in a line with us. The moment they do so we can complete boycott of foreign cloth inside of six months. The programme definitely therefore has to be this:

We leave Indian mills severely alone. We carry on a whirlwind campaign for boycott of foreign cloth through Khadi, asking people to count no sacrifice too great in adopting Khadi. We must have faith in ourselves and in our people and believe that they can make this which appears to me to be small sacrifice. But I confess that at the present moment I do not visualize the organization that is needed to carry on the boycott. The political who are in a possession of the platform do not mean to do any serious business. They will not concentrate on any constructive work. Jawahar in a letter truly describes the atmosphere, when he says: 'There is violence in the air.' We read and hear so much about the boycott of British cloth in Bengal, but the letters I receive almost every week show that there is no real boycott. There is no organization behind it, there is no will working behind it. All things considered what will you advise me to do.

The expected letter from Romain Rolland is due next Tuesday at the latest. I must after that come to a decision quickly. Supposing that Romain Rolland predisposes me in favour of the European visit, what would you have me to do in view of the talk of the boycott. Would you want me for the sake of the boycott not to go to Europe? I shall accept your decision whatever it may be. I am not personally keen on the European visit, but if all is plain sailing in India and if Romain Rolland wants me to visit Europe, I should feel bound to accept the European invitations. Will you please wire your decision? Jawahar will be with you and probably you will know Doctor Ansari's mind.

Yours sincerely

12

To Hermann Kallenbach

Hermann Kallenbach (1871–1945) was a German doctor who became one of Gandhiji's closest friends in South Africa.

Nandi Hills,
[Near Bengaluru]
13 May, 1927

As I lie in bed and look up old undisposed of correspondence and revive old and sacred memories, I chance upon your letter of 27th February sent with Andrews' letter from your home at Inanda, and I revive so many pleasant and sacred memories. Every letter that you have written during the last two years—and you have not written many, has been a despondent letter, distressful of yourself; but as long as I live I am not going to lose faith in you. I am hoping that someday as before you will have a fatigue of the exciting things that gives you momentary pleasure and that you will at least come to India to meet an old friend and renew many old acquaintances. You have made a provisional promise to do so next September or October. Do come if you can and then stay as long as you like or as little as you like.

I am glad you are having short spells of Andrews' company. I have not come across a humbler or more god-fearing man throughout my varied experience.

You don't want me to say anything about my illness; because I see you do get *Young India* and read it. I am at the present moment taking my cure on a little hill in the State of Mysore where an army of devoted volunteers and many of my closest co-workers are looking after me. Mrs Gandhi and Devdas are with me. The names of others would mean nothing to you. So I do not give them. But when you do come, you will see them all and recognize them as having been with me on this hill.

This loss of strength came in the twinkling of an eye. Latterly I had put such terrific strain upon the brain that I was afraid of a crisis and it came just when I was arranging to have a lighter programme. But God seemed to say 'I shall demolish your pride before you recognize your mad method and show you that you were utterly wrong in rushing as you have been doing thinking that it was all well because it was for a good cause. You fool you thought that you would work wonders. Have your lesson now and learn whilst there is yet time that God alone is to wonder work and He uses whom He pleases as His instrument.' I am taking the chastisement I hope in due humility and if He raises me from this sick bed, I am making Him promises that I shall reform my ways and shall seek still more strenuously to know His will unto it.

I hope you are keeping in touch with Manilal. He has got a girl with a strong character as his wife. She is the best girl I could possibly have found for him. Chance put her my way. She belongs to godly family. Remember you are one of the trustees for Phoenix and I look to you to discharge your trust.

Sastri will be in South Africa probably within a month of your receipt of this. I have had long chats with him about you and your associations with Gokhale. Do try to be closely to him and bring all our old companions in touch with him.

Yours sincerely,
M.K. Gandhi

13

To Gulzarilal Nanda

From an early age, Gulzarilal Nanda (1898–1998) was influenced by Gandhian ideals and thoughts, prompting him to join the freedom movement. Though cautioned by Gandhiji about the hardships of such a life, he went ahead regardless. He went on to become interim Prime Minister of India on two occasions.

To Gulzarilal Nanda
Nandi Hills,
28 May, 1927

My Dear Gulzarilal,

I was delighted to hear from you. Whilst lying on my bed, I have constantly thought of so many like you in whom I am deeply interested and from whom, I expect many large and big things if only God will give them the requisite health for the task before them.

Your description of a truly religious life is accurate. I have not a shadow of a doubt that this blessed state of inward joy and freedom from anxiety should last in the midst of the greatest trials conceivable. It admits of no exception whatsoever. Naturally, it is unattainable except by the very fewest. But that it is attainable by human beings, I have also no doubt. That we do not find in history evidence regarding the existence of any such person merely proves to me all the record that we have has been prepared by imperfect beings, and it is impossible for imperfect beings to give us a faithful record of perfect ones. The same may be said of our own experiences. We have to be very nearly perfect in order to meet perfect souls such as you have described. Nor need you think that I have laid down an absurd proposition inasmuch as it is incapable of being recorded, or being experienced by the average man. To raise such a doubt would be begging the question, for we are here picturing to ourselves extraordinary mortals, though mortals nevertheless, and surely extraordinary powers are required to find out these extraordinary mortals. This statement is true even of much lesser things, things almost ridiculous. And yet very difficult of accomplishment, such, for instance, as, the discoveries of Sir J.C. Bose or the finest paintings. Both these, we average beings will have to take on trust. It is only the privileged few who have got the special faculty for understanding and appreciating either those discoveries, or those paintings. These do not appear to us to be incredible and we are able to accept them on faith only because in favour of these we have the testimony of a larger number of witnesses than we can possibly have for the things of permanent value, such as human perfection of the utmost type. Therefore the limitation that you have accepted is quite a workable thing for the time being. For, even inside the limitation, there is ample scope for widening the field for the progress of the state of being and remaining unruffled in the face of the onslaught of sorrows and trials, which before regeneration would have paralysed us.

I am glad you have intensified your devotions. I do not know what you are reading at present. And I do not know whether I told you that we must arrive at a time when we do not need the solace of many books but that we make one book yield us all we want. In the last stage, of course, when life becomes one of perfect surrender and complete self-effacement, the support of even one book becomes unnecessary. At the present moment, though I am reading many things, Bhagavad Gita is becoming more and more the only infallible guide, the only dictionary of reference, in which I find all the sorrows, all the troubles, all the trials arranged in the alphabetical order with exquisite solutions. I think I did tell you that *The Song Celestial* was the best rendering I had come across of the Bhagavad Gita. But if you do not know Sanskrit, I know that a knowledge of Sanskrit to enable you to understand Bhagavad Gita is easily within your power. You can almost in a month's time know enough Sanskrit to understand the original text. For, though the English rendering is grand and though you might be able to get some Hindi or Urdu translation also, of course there is nothing like the original. The original will enable you to give your own meaning and gloss to the text. That book is not a historical record, but it is a record of the concrete experience of its author, whether it was really Vyas or not I am not concerned. And if it is a record of anybody's experience, it must not be beyond us to be able to test the truth of it by repeating the experience. I am testing the truth almost every day in my life and find it never failing. This of course does not mean that I have reached the state described, for instance, at the end of the Second Chapter. But I know that the more we carry out the prescription given in it, the nearer do we answer the description given of the perfect state.

I hope you are keeping good health. I am of course making steady progress.

Yours sincerely,

14

To Kailas Nath Katju

Kailas Nath Katju (1887–1968) was an eminent jurist and Congress leader who went on to become Governor of Orissa (now Odisha) and then Governor of West Bengal. He was also Chief Minister of Madhya Pradesh.

To Dr Kailas Nath Katju,
Gudiatham (South India),
1 September, 1927

Dear Friend,

My weakness of body is my excuse for dictating this letter. But for that weakness I would have gladly written myself. I thank you for your letter and the first instalment of your contribution to Khadi. Your letter is so good and is likely to influence others. If you have no objection, I would like to publish that part of it which relates to Khadi. But please do not hesitate to refuse permission, if you would on any account not like the publication of the letter, whether with or without your name.

As for the black alpaca chapkan concerned, give me an order and I can have for you one made of very fine black Khadi. It looks as good as alpaca. You may not know that in Madras many advocates and Vakils wear Khaddar chapkans even when they do not use Khadi for other articles of dress and as it so happens, the Khaddar chapkans, the poor practitioners find to be suitable because of their comparative cheapness. In your case I may not think of cheapness at all. If you give the order, I am not going to secure for you the cheapest but the most expensive and the most elegant.

Now a word about personal spinning. I quite agree with you that love of Khaddar need not include personal spinning. But love of the starving millions does, for two reasons: First, because, personal spinning renews our daily bond with them. Secondly, by personally spinning each known member of society creates a spinning atmosphere which makes it easier for workers to induce the unwilling, because unbelieving, villagers to take to hand-spinning. I would like to add a third reason which I know you would not despise. Every yard of well-spun yarn adds to the wealth of the country, be the addition ever so infinitesimal. You know what the lawyers do, so often whilst awaiting their turn in the law courts. They either play with their pencils or with their paper-tape or worse still open out their little penknives and fidget with the edges of the desks at which they are sitting. I wonder if I could induce you to take up the little takli which could be made of silver, gold or ivory if you like, and put in a delicate little cylinder. Takli-spinning is easily learnt. Will you take to it? It will be, I know, laughed at in the beginning; then it will cease to attract notice one way or the other and if you could go through the two stages and persist, it will be copied by others. I hope you do not resent my saying all this to you. You have given me an inch with hearty goodwill and you must not be surprised if I now ask for more.

Yes, indeed, I demanded great sacrifices from lawyers. But looking back to 1920 and '21, I feel that I asked for nothing very extraordinary and I feel that I had a right to demand the largest measure of sacrifice from those to whose profession I once belonged.

The little ones now consider themselves, to be too big to sit in my lap. Please, however, tell them that whenever

I meet them again, I am going to make them pay for still remembering me.

I am passing your cheque for Rs 100 to the Treasurer of the All-India Spinners' Association.

Yours sincerely,
M.K. Gandhi

15

To Winston Churchill

Gandhi's response to the stated desire of Winston Churchill (1874-1964), the Prime Minister of the United Kingdom during World War II, of 'crushing' the 'half-naked' 'seditious fakir'.

Dilkusha,
Panchagani,
17 July, 1944

Dear Prime Minister,

You are reported to have the desire to crush the 'naked fakir', as you are said to have described me. I have been long trying to be a fakir and that, naked—a more difficult task. I therefore regard the expression as a compliment though unintended. I approach you then as such and ask you to trust and use me for the sake of your people and mine and through them those of the world.

Your sincere friend,
M.K. Gandhi

16

To Sardar Patel

Gandhiji wrote this letter to Sardar Patel at a time when the country was about to witness great changes. Bapu urged Patel to keep himself abreast of the numerous happenings across the country, and demanded that he himself be kept informed of the same.

To Sardar Vallabhbhai Patel
Shrirampur,
25 December, 1946

Chi. Vallabhbhai,

Your letter to Pyarelal reached me direct yesterday. Pyarelal and all the rest are engrossed in their own work and are staking their lives.... So Pyarelal does not know about this letter. He comes to see me occasionally and will read it when he comes here next.

I am dictating this at 3 a.m. I shall have a wash at 4 a.m. and prayers after that. This is the present routine. I shall carry on only if such is God's will. However there is nothing in my health which should make you anxious. The body responds to the demands made upon it, but it is a real ordeal for me. My truth and non-violence are being weighed in a balance which is much more accurate than any a pearl merchant ever used. It is so sensitive as to register the difference of even the hundredth fraction of a hair. They in themselves can never be found wanting. If anything is to be found wanting, it may be I who have constituted myself their representative; if so, I at least hope that God will take me away and work through some other worthier agent. I am sorry that I cannot myself do the work which Pyarelal used to do for me and I have not yet been able to prepare the two men who are with me to do it. But both are intelligent. I therefore hope to be able to arrange it. In this your letter will afford me encouragement. Jaisukhlal left Manu at her own wish three or four days ago. I allowed her to come, as she was prepared to stay and die with me if necessary. And now I am dictating this to her, lying down with my eyes closed so as to reduce my exertion to the minimum. Sucheta [Kripalani] is also in this room. She is still asleep....

The telegram you sent me is fit only to be thrown into the waste-paper basket. There is no limit to exaggeration here. Not that the people exaggerate intentionally; they simply do not know what exaggeration means. The imagination of the people runs riot like the local vegetation which presses in on all sides. All around us I find huge coconut and betelnut palms, and a large variety of greens grow in their shade. The rivers are all like the Sindhu, the Ganga, the Yamuna and the Brahmaputra. These empty their waters in the Bay of Bengal. My advice is that if you have not replied to him already you should ask the man who sent the telegram to you to furnish proof for his statements so that 'the Central Government may try to do something about it, though they have no power to interfere in terms of the Constitution'. And add: 'Gandhi is there in your midst and it is impossible that he would not hear you. But he is an apostle of truth and non-violence and therefore there is a possibility of his disappointing you. But if he disappoints you, how can we, who were trained under him, hope to satisfy you? But we shall do what we can.' Don't tell anyone that since Gandhi is there, he need not bring his problems to you. Let him write to you as well, and it would be your duty to afford relief to him even by going against me, for that is what I have taught you. The situation is difficult. Truth is nowhere to be found. Violence masquerades as non-violence, irreligion as religion. But truth and non-violence can be tested only in such conditions, I know; that is why I am here. Do not call me away. If I ran away in fear, that would be my own misfortune; but India is certainly not so unlucky. I am here to do or die. News came over the radio yesterday that Jawaharlal, Kripalani and Deo were coming to have consultations with me. That is enough.

What is the use of my meeting everyone? However, if any one among you wants to ask me anything, he can.

What I wrote about Assam was not meant for immediate publication. But rest assured that I am right on that point.

You will have seen the report of the Bihar [Muslim] League. I wrote to Rajendrababu about it and have asked him to acquaint all of you with my views. I have also written to the Bihar Chief Minister. Even if half of what the report says is correct, it is bad business. I have no doubt that an impartial commission of inquiry with which no one can find any fault ought to be set up without a single day's delay. Whatever is correct in the allegations must be admitted straightaway and the rest should be referred to the commission. You should also discuss this with your Muslim League colleagues in the Cabinet. I am still in correspondence with Suhrawardy. When it is completed I shall send it all to you. Jawaharlal will see what has passed between us so far.

If you are not doing it already, please read the summary of my post-prayer speeches which is sent to the newspapers. Or go through the cuttings which Mani could give you. I know the high pressure under which you are working, but some things have to be done in spite of this pressure. To keep abreast of what I am saying is one of them.

I do not think I can hope that your health is excellent, but trust that it is good enough for you to work. I think it can be very much improved. I would still ask you to call Dinshah [Mehta] in for treatment. I have no doubt that he is a good and sincere man with a benevolent outlook on life. What if he is not so efficient? You ask about Sushila. I cannot say she is in good health. She is at her post in inhospitable villages and is doing good work. Even a quack is a rarity in these parts; so naturally the people make much of someone like her. Therefore do not be anxious about any of us here. And when every one of them is here to die, their falling ill should not be of great concern. If they die, it would be a master for congratulation. For this they have to die in purity.

Blessings,
Bapu

17

To Abdul Ghaffar Khan

Khan Abdul Ghaffar Khan (1890–1988), also known as the Frontier Gandhi for his non-violent and Gandhian ideals, was a force to reckon with in the North-West Frontier Province. Mahatma Gandhi was particularly worried about his health and his well-being, since he believed that Ghaffar Khan lived under a lot of threats. This letter is reflective of his concerns for Badshah Khan.

To Abdul Ghaffar Khan
Bhangi Colony,
New Delhi,
5 July, 1947

Dear Badshah,

Khudai Khidmatgar Alam Khan saw me before 12 o'clock and he said that he was leaving for Peshawar tonight. I did not send any letter through him. But I told him that there should be no demonstration against the Muslim League, that it should be enough that in the present state of tension and misrepresentation Khudai Khidmatgars should not vote at all one way or the other, that they were entitled so far as internal affairs were concerned to claim and to have complete autonomy without any interference from Pakistan or the Union, and that they could come to a decision as to the choice between the Union or Pakistan when the constitutions of the two were promulgated and when the Frontier Province had fashioned its own autonomous constitution. Above all, every occasion for clash with the Muslim League members was to be avoided.

Real Pathan bravery was now on its trial. It was to be shown by cheerfully meeting blows or even meeting death at the hands of the opponents without the slightest sort of retaliation. Boycott would certainly result in a legal victory for Pakistanis, but it would be a moral defeat, if without the slightest fear of violence from your side, the bulk of Pathans refrained in a dignified manner from participating in the referendum. There should be no fuss, no procession, and no disobedience of any orders from the authority.

I had acted promptly on receipt of your letter. I wrote a long letter to His Excellency on which he took action. You must have seen also how I had dealt with the question of the Frontier Province in one of my post- prayer speeches. I send you herewith a copy of my letter to the Viceroy and of my post-prayer speech. This letter is also in answer to a complaint received by the Viceroy that it was reported that there was fear of disturbance to be caused by the Khudai Khidmatgars.

I hope the strain under which you are working is not telling upon your health.

Love,
Bapu